# Mentoring for Ministry

# Mentoring for Ministry

## The Grace of Growing Pastors

Edited by
CRAIG T. KOCHER,
JASON BYASSEE,
and JAMES C. HOWELL

CASCADE *Books* · Eugene, Oregon

MENTORING FOR MINISTRY
The Grace of Growing Pastors

Copyright © 2017 Wipf and Stock Publishers. All rights reserved. Except for brief quotations in critical publications or reviews, no part of this book may be reproduced in any manner without prior written permission from the publisher. Write: Permissions, Wipf and Stock Publishers, 199 W. 8th Ave., Suite 3, Eugene, OR 97401.

Cascade Books
An Imprint of Wipf and Stock Publishers
199 W. 8th Ave., Suite 3
Eugene, OR 97401

www.wipfandstock.com

PAPERBACK ISBN: 978-1-4982-2855-8
HARDCOVER ISBN: 978-1-4982-2857-2
EBOOK ISBN: 978-1-4982-2856-5

*Cataloguing-in-Publication data:*

Names: Kocher, Craig T., editor. | Byassee, Jason, editor. | Howell, James C., 1955–, editor.

Title: Mentoring for ministry : the grace of growing pastors / edited by Craig T. Kocher, Jason Byassee, and James C. Howell.

Description: Eugene, OR : Cascade Books, 2017 | Includes bibliographical references.

Identifiers: ISBN 978-1-4982-2855-8 (paperback) | ISBN 978-1-4982-2857-2 (hardcover) | ISBN 978-1-4982-2856-5 (ebook)

Subjects: LCSH: Mentoring—Religious aspects—Christianity.

Classification: BV4408.5 .M46 2017 (paperback) | BV4408.5 .M46 (ebook)

Manufactured in the U.S.A.                                    05/17/17

To Abby, Jaylynn, and Lisa
Mentors in life; partners in ministry

# Contents

# Introduction

EVERY CREATED THING HAS a beginning. This project has its origin in the mentoring relationships between its three editors, which explains the somewhat parochial nature of its collection of authors—centered as we are in North Carolina Methodism. These mentoring relationships started long before we knew what a "mentor" was and before a few of us knew what a Christian was.

We did, however, know what a basketball was. Barely. The first basketball team I, Jason, ever played on was a youth team coached by one Jim Kocher. My teammate was his elder son, Keith Kocher. And the annoying little brother who wouldn't get out of our practice drills was one Craig Kocher. We lost every game, went 0–11 (and so maybe should have let Craig play—how much worse could it have been?). Later Keith and I redeemed that winless season with an undefeated one, but that's another story. Craig went on to work as a sports broadcaster for a time, including being the voice of the UNC women's basketball team, before switching lanes and becoming my fellow student at Duke Divinity School, where we prepared for ministry in the United Methodist Church.

I'd gotten there under James Howell's tutelage, as I discuss in my chapter. And when Craig was graduating from Duke, looking for a job, James was asking who the best students were coming out of divinity school for his open associate's position. This is one trait of good mentors—they're on the hunt for great talent, not for their project alone, but for the church at large (Leighton Ford discusses this trait in his autobiographical essay). I remember Craig and I trekking to Davidson to hear James and consider whether he should work for him. Davidson UMC's bell choir had a lovely song that came up, surprisingly, during James' sermon. It was a trick, of the sort preachers know they're not above, even though our professor colleagues seem to frown on that sort of thing. I liked it. Craig was puzzled. We mentees can be tough.

Craig worked for James before becoming an associate also for Will Willimon and Sam Wells at Duke Chapel, making Craig officially the best mentored minister in Methodism, maybe in all of Christendom. And he has not wasted this gift. He has sent hundreds of students into ministry while at Davidson, Duke, and now the University of Richmond. The annoying little kid knows how to spot talent, befriend younger people, be open to criticism himself, and set it loose. He's a mentor, as all Christian leaders ought to be.

Most of these authors share a branch on this family tree, beginning with James. Some are fellow travelers in different settings, such as Prince, pastoring a crucial Baptist church in Winston-Salem, Ken, pastoring Tenth Church in Vancouver, Sam Wells, who is vicar of St. Martin in the Fields in London, and a highly visible voice on both sides of the Atlantic. Martin Marty has supervised hundreds of doctoral students at the University of Chicago. When I met Marty at a party for *Christian Century* staff he immediately dropped all interest in everyone but my one-year old son. He hoisted him up, produced a gold watch on a chain, and immediately mesmerized him. Who was this strong bald man with the open face and cool toys and even more love than intellect? Later, Marty counseled me at a career intersection that John Winthrop, pilgrim divine, spoke of a language with which God writes on the heart, that each of us has to discern. It was counsel biblical, sage, and true: he couldn't read that secret writing, only I could. But I was not alone.

Several authors have also gotten to work with James, such as Melanie. One got to grow up in James' house. Sarah Howell is one of the most promising young pastors we have, whom we all remember when she was tiny (but not annoying that I recall). She's doing things none of us could do with her Roots Revival service in Winston-Salem, opening the question of how it is that we mentors can guide someone so very different from us who can do things we never could, and reminding us how quickly the mentee becomes the mentor. We get credit—don't we?! Others are colleagues we admire at peer institutions, like Elaine Heath, who has marked mentoring as a key trait of post-Christendom forms of church, and is now putting her prodigious talents to work as dean of Duke Divinity School. Others have been fellow travelers without mentoring or being mentored by any of us but by serving countless others nearby, like Leighton and Jeremy. Jeremy still leads this way from his little parish in the mountains after directing Duke's rural church institute for years. Small rural churches have been Methodism's strength since, well, there was something called Methodism. These communities are under more duress than ever. And Jeremy insisted he pastor in one of them.

So there's a sort of parochial origin to this collection, but there's a parochial origin to Christianity. God calls one couple, Abram and Sarai, to people God's family and renew the world. God calls one peasant girl, Mary, to be mother of God. God gets born someplace specific, to bless all other specific places. Will Willimon tells a story of a Yale professor handing him cassette tapes of great preachers in America. Will listened. "What'd you notice?" the mentor asked. "They all have accents," responded the young South Carolina preacher, out of water in New Haven, Connecticut. "Good. Now stop being embarrassed by yours." We editors here speak with accents southern and Methodist, though we've grown up and gotten out a little, been graced with friends from elsewhere, and learned to befriend those whose accents vary a great deal. We all came from somewhere. God did too. That's why God can use any of us to bless somebody else. We hope God has with this book.

Jason Byassee

# Contributors

**Jason Byassee**, Teaches preaching and Bible at Vancouver Theological Seminary. He is a fellow in Theology and Leadership at Duke Divinity School and previously served as Senior Pastor of Boone United Methodist Church in Boone, North Carolina.

**Melanie L. Dobson**, Minister of Faith Formation, Myers Park United Methodist Church, Charlotte, North Carolina. She is the author of *Health as a Virtue: Thomas Aquinas and the Practice of Habits of Health.*

**Leighton Ford**, President, Leighton Ford Ministries, which focuses on raising up young people to spread the message of Christ worldwide.

**Elaine Heath**, Dean, Duke Divinity School. She is the author of several books on Christian ministry and evangelism, and is a founder of the Missional Wisdom Foundation.

**James C. Howell**, Senior Pastor of Myers Park United Methodist Church, Charlotte, North Carolina. He is the author of numerous books on faith and ministry.

**Sarah S. Howell**, Associate Minister, Centenary United Methodist Church, Winston-Salem, North Carolina. She leads Roots Revival, a midweek service grounded in Americana/roots-based music.

**Craig T. Kocher**, University Chaplain and Jessie Ball duPont Chair of the Chaplaincy at the University of Richmond. He previously pastored churches in North Carolina and served as Associate Dean of Duke University Chapel.

# Contributors

**Martin E. Marty**, Fairfax M. Cone Distinguished Service Professor Emeritus, University of Chicago, where he taught in the Divinity School and History Department. The author of more than sixty books, Dr. Marty is an ordained Lutheran pastor.

**Prince Rivers**, Senior Pastor of United Metropolitan Missionary Baptist Church, Winston-Salem, North Carolina.

**Ken Shigematsu**, Senior Pastor, Tenth Church, Vancouver, British Columbia. He is the author of the international bestseller, *God in My Everything*.

**Jeremy Troxler**, Pastor of Spruce Pine United Methodist Church, Spruce Pine, North Carolina. He previously served as director of the Thriving Rural Communities Initiative at Duke Divinity School.

**Samuel Wells**, Vicar of St Martin-in-the-Fields, London. The author of many books on theology and ministry, he previously served as Dean of Duke University Chapel and Research Professor of Christian ethics at Duke Divinity School.

# *Chapter 1*

# Mentoring the Mother of God

JEREMY TROXLER

## PRELUDE: THE MAKING OF A MENTOR

[Zechariah's] wife was a descendant of Aaron, and her name was Elizabeth. Both of them were righteous before God, living blamelessly according to all the commandments of regulations of the Lord . . .

LUKE 1:5–6

THE JOURNEY TO THE manger begins with the making of a mentor.

Elizabeth had grown up the child of a family of priests. Now she was a veteran clergy spouse, her life having been poured into the mold of temple piety and shaped into something holy. Luke says that both Elizabeth and her husband Zechariah were just and righteous before God, walking in God's ways and keeping the commandments of Scripture.

Elizabeth was faithful, a person of good character.

Perhaps that character had also been forged by the suffering Elizabeth had endured. As the wife of a priest she lived in a public fishbowl, her words and deeds scrutinized by murmuring gossips who held priestly families to a higher standard of holiness. Perhaps being put on a pedestal made Elizabeth's failure to have children all the more humiliating. She and Zechariah had tried to get pregnant for years, but after countless monthly disappointments and several devastating miscarriages, the nursery remained empty and silent. So at the barber shop or the hair salon the village folk shook their heads in pity and said "Bless her heart" whenever the subject of poor Elizabeth came up. They wondered in whispers what secret sins the priest's wife must have committed to have suffered from a barren womb: as if her worth as a woman were determined by nothing more than a fertility test.

Now crow's feet cracked around Elizabeth's eyes. Rivulets of wrinkles trickled across her face. Her only fruitfulness was the spread of graying hair. Elizabeth was "advanced in years." But she was also advanced in soul. Her prayers and her worship had grooved a well-worn path between earth and heaven. Her pain had tenderized Elizabeth's heart and her works of mercy had carved her character. She carried about her the hard-won wisdom of a thousand tiny daily internal and external battles fought and won, or at least endured.

She was, in short, holy. And perhaps, lonely.

Suddenly, the angelic messenger Gabriel jumps Zechariah in the sanctuary, announces that Zeke is the new Abram and Elizabeth is the new Sarai, and then pushes the mute button on the disbelieving old priest's tongue.

Soon thereafter Elizabeth conceives. The Lord has "looked favorably upon her." God's grace erases the disgrace of human beings. Meaning is given to her suffering, as in a moment years of patient but profitless prayer are re-narrated as prelude and preparation. Elizabeth has been readied to raise a prophet.

She has also been given three of the chief pre-requisites for becoming a mentor: a life worthy of imitation, a wisdom worthy of being shared, and a character to which another's well-being can be trusted.

Those pre-requisites will soon prove essential, because Elizabeth is about to become not only the mother of John the Baptist, but the mentor to the mother of God. She will serve as the forerunner of Mary even as her own son John will one day pave the path for Mary's son Jesus.

Elizabeth becomes the exemplar and patron saint of faithful mentoring offered in the name of Christ.


## HOW THIS CAN BE

Mary said to the angel, "How can this be . . . ?"

LUKE 1:34

Christian tradition often speaks of Mary the mother of Jesus as the *theotokos*, or "God-bearer." As one who says "Yes" to the will of God and who carries the life of Christ within her, Mary is often thought of as a model for all Christians who seek to be "God-bearers" and "Christ-carriers" in the world.[1]

But Mary will not carry Christ into the world alone. The journey to the manger began with the making of her mentor, Elizabeth. Before the angelic messenger Gabriel breaks the good news of Mary's chosen-ness to her, he has first arranged for Mary to have a faithful guide and companion: an elder who is a little further along in life and who has experienced some of what she herself is about to experience. Luke makes the connection between the two callings explicit: he describes Gabriel's visit to Nazareth as unfolding according to the timetable of Elizabeth's first two trimesters, "in the sixth month."

Elizabeth's and Mary's parallel pregnancies are thus not two separate stories but two converging branches of one act of God.

When Gabriel greets Mary as the favored one and announces that she will give birth to the Son of the Most High, the wonder-struck, teenage Mary asks Gabriel, "How can this be, since I am a virgin?" Behind this query about obstetric mechanics are perhaps other, unspoken questions: "How can this be, that the life of God might be found within *me*?" "How can this be that I, unworthy as I am, can be a vessel of the Christ?"

Gabriel's response is to point Mary to another who has experienced God's surprising calling and dumbfounding grace: "And now, your relative Elizabeth in her old age has also conceived a son; and this is the sixth month for her who was said to be barren. For nothing will be impossible with God" (Luke 1:36–37).

Gabriel ministers to Mary's doubts and insecurities by pointing to another human life claimed for divine purposes and says, "God has done this kind of thing before." Hearing the story of Elizabeth cements and emboldens Mary's "Here I am, a servant of the Lord."

From the beginning of Luke's Gospel, then, the call to be a God-bearer is yoked with the call to seek a mentor. Salvation will be arranged like the animals on Noah's ark: two by two.

How can this be, that we, like Mary, might become instruments of God's salvation? By the grace of having and being mentors.

---

1. Dean and Foster, *God-Bearing Life.*

## THE JOURNEY TO THE HILL COUNTRY

In those days Mary set out and went with haste to a Judean town in the hill country, where she entered the house of Zechariah and greeted Elizabeth.

LUKE 1:39–40

Gabriel's visit leads Mary to pack her bags and join a caravan to make her own visit to Elizabeth. Luke says that Mary sets out on her journey "with haste," with a sense of urgency and purpose. Maybe a few days have passed, and Mary wonders if the calling she has discerned was all just a kind of dream: so she is anxious to see if the angel's description of Elizabeth's pregnancy proves true. Maybe Mary has told her parents she is "in the family way," and they are so angry they have either kicked her out or decided together that she needs to get away from the village for a while, rather than have the bump appear and become the source of town gossip. Or maybe Mary is just a pregnant teenager who is scared to death and needs to talk with a good, wise, older friend—especially one who knows what it feels like to have been touched by a miracle.

So Mary sets out for the hill country. In this story, at least, the responsibility for finding a mentor rests upon the one who is seeking guidance. Mary is the one who must purposefully seek out Elizabeth.

There are no doubt many things that potential mentors can do to nurture mentoring relationships with those taking their first steps in ministry. They can notice which students or interns or new colleagues seem particularly desirous of learning from them, and can invite them to share lunch or a cup of coffee to get to know them better. They can create spaces where deeper relationship might happen. Perhaps Mary and Elizabeth have met before, and in their interactions Elizabeth showed a genuine interest in her younger relative.

And yet the final door to an authentic mentoring relationship must be unlocked by the mentee. He or she must admit relative ignorance and be willing to learn from another, must make a decision to seek the potential mentor's counsel and friendship. The mentee is required to move past a desire to impress a role model or find self-esteem-boosting affirmation from an authority figure to make him or herself vulnerable to genuine growth.

Sometimes in seminary field education a divinity student will gain valuable experience by working at a church under the tutelage of an experienced pastoral supervisor. Often the relationship between supervisor and intern grows into a mentoring relationship. And yet there is a difference between serving as a supervisor and being a mentor. One is an assigned role; the other is a form of relationship. All field-education pastors serve as supervisors; some will become mentors as well. No matter what a supervisor might do that may appear mentor-like, mentors are ultimately anointed in the heart of the mentee. It takes two to form an authentic mentoring relationship. A supervisor cannot self-appoint him or herself a mentor to the intern, barraging the student with war stories, unsolicited advice, and probing questions out of an unhealthy desire to be looked-up-to by a younger colleague. An invitation to deeper relationship may be offered, but the development of a true mentoring relationship cannot be forced: it must arise organically out of the experience of working or learning together. While such a relationship can be fostered, it is more often discovered, received as a surprising gift of grace.

Mary must be the one who sets out to make the journey to Elizabeth. Mary must be the one to enter the house. Mary must offer the first word of greeting.

The next step lies with Elizabeth.


## ELIZABETH'S JOYFUL WELCOME AND BLESSING

When Elizabeth heard Mary's greeting, the child leaped in her womb. And Elizabeth was filled with the Holy Spirit and exclaimed with a loud cry, "Blessed are you among women, and blessed is the fruit of your womb. And why has this happened to me, that the mother of my Lord comes to me? For as soon as I heard the sound of your greeting, the child in my womb leaped for joy. And blessed is she who believed that there would be a fulfillment of what was spoken to her by the Lord."

LUKE 1:41–45

Mary's perhaps tentative greeting is met by Elizabeth's extravagant hospitality and compassionate spiritual sensitivity. Surely Elizabeth has a great deal on her own mind. She is concerned about Zechariah's dumbness and anxious over her own high-risk pregnancy. And yet Elizabeth stops what she is doing and focuses her whole attention upon the young woman who has entered her door. She allows herself to be interrupted by Mary—and thus allows herself to be interrupted by God.[2] She makes it clear to Mary that she is glad to see her, that Mary's visit is not an added burden but a surprising gift. In this Elizabeth shows a genuine humility of spirit, the older woman humbling herself before the younger: "And why has this happened to me, that the mother of my Lord comes to *me*?" (Luke 1:43).

Elizabeth makes Mary feel for a moment as if she were the most important person in the world: which of course, she might actually be.

Elizabeth's welcome is the overflow of her generous soul. A lifetime of keeping the commandments and daily welcoming God's presence into her life now enables her to welcome the God-bearer into her home. Elizabeth's life of faithfulness has also given her a certain spiritual sensitivity that allows her to utter just the right word to Mary for just the right time.

Elizabeth will astonish her visitor with the depth of her welcome and her ability to discern at first glance the reason for Mary's arrival. Luke attributes Elizabeth's perspicacity to the filling of the Holy Spirit. Perhaps a lifetime of listening to others and of listening for the Spirit of the Lord has also given her the ears to hear what is behind both the inflection in Mary's greeting and the umbilical hallelujah of little John.

Faithful mentors like Elizabeth have open doors and open ears.

Elizabeth not only has the ears to hear the word of the Lord, but the tongue to speak it. She offers a timely and true word that shows her to be just as much a prophet as her baby boy. She practically shouts with joy as she greets Mary with words that echo Gabriel's "Hail, favored one!": "Blessed are you among women, and blessed is the fruit of your womb!" (Luke 1:42).

Elizabeth doesn't patronize Mary as a sweet naïve girl or a cute young thing, but treats her with the utmost seriousness, as more than an equal. Her words demonstrate great sensitivity to the needs of Mary's trembling soul.

Due to her scandalous pregnancy, many of the words Mary has heard recently have likely been curse words. "Pitied are you," others may have communicated to Mary. Now Elizabeth splashes beatitude all over her instead. "Blessed are you," she pronounces. "You are not a failure or an embarrassment or an object of charity, you are a blessing. And blessed is your baby. This baby is not a mistake or a "whoops" or a burden, this baby is a blessing. And blessed are you for having trusted God. You are blessed, blessed, blessed."

---

2. Bonhoeffer, *Life Together*, 99.

The modern not-yet-canonized saint Jean Vanier has given his life to living with and loving and learning from persons with developmental disabilities. Vanier's experiences have led him to conclude, "To Love is not to give of your riches but to reveal to others their riches, their gifts, their value; and to trust them in their capacity to grow. To love someone is to show to them their beauty, their worth and their importance."[3]

Elizabeth loves Mary in that sense. She knows that Mary needs encouragement as she takes these first nervous steps in following God's call. So Elizabeth glows over her, gushes over her, makes a fuss over her. She shows Mary her own beauty, worth, importance, that she is blessed, blessed, blessed.

And yet Elizabeth also understands that Mary's pregnancy is not just about Mary, but about God. Elizabeth sees God's fingerprints all over Mary's life, and simply points to the evidence. Elizabeth knows that the purpose of Mary's visit is not wish-fulfillment, or self-fulfillment, but faith-fulfillment. So she doesn't name Mary as "talented" or "special," but as "blessed." She also encourages Mary to trust in God's promise to her: "And blessed is she who believed there would be a fulfillment of what was spoken to her by the Lord!" (Luke 1:45).

The practice of mentoring is not merely an end in itself, two persons celebrating how fortunate they are to have found each other. Mentoring happens when two persons empower each other to more deeply trust in the faithfulness of their common Lord.

Notice that in her words Elizabeth does not provide any new information to Mary, beyond the revelation of John's gynecological gyrations. Everything else Elizabeth communicates to her guest is something that Mary likely already knows. And yet hearing someone else speak her own truth aloud will have a profound impact upon Mary: the internal, personal experience of call longs to hear itself echoed externally in the confirmation offered by another.

After leading a prayer retreat for a group of college students, Henri Nouwen wondered in his diary what he really had to offer such bright young people. "The remarks by the students about prayer were beautiful and full of meaning. Only they themselves did not know it," he wrote. "When I went home last night, I thought, 'What do I have to say to these men and women who are so earnest in their search for God and live such good lives?'"[4]

3. Vanier, *Broken Body*, 37.
4. Nouwen, *Genesee Diary*, 161.

There can be heard here an echo of Elizabeth's glorious bewilderment in her question to Mary, a question asked by every self-aware mentor: "Why have you come to *me*?" But Henri Nouwen records a moment of insight in his diary. "I realized," he wrote, "that the only thing I have to do is to say loudly what they already know in their hearts so that they can recognize it as really theirs and affirm it in gratitude."[5]

Elizabeth (literally) says loudly what Mary knows in her heart to be true, so that Mary can claim it as her own and affirm it in gratitude. The best mentors leak contagious joy from their lives: they display a sense of humor and a gaiety of demeanor that have about them the rollicking freedom of resurrection.

Mary, the favored one, is not the only person full of grace in this story. Elizabeth is full of grace as well, because joyful hospitality is a special case of grace: a gift given that has not been earned.

The welcome offered by a mentor is an act of grace. And grace makes human beings sing.

## SPACE FOR THE SOUL TO SING

And Mary said,
My soul magnifies the Lord,
and my spirit rejoices in God my Savior,
For he has looked with favor on the lowliness of his servant . . .

LUKE 1:46–48

Elizabeth's beatitudes over her prompt Mary to sing an impromptu freedom song known as the Magnificat:[6] "My soul magnifies the Lord, and my spirit rejoices in God my Savior . . ." Elizabeth has looked upon Mary with favor, and such benediction enables her to perceive the gracious gaze of her Lord, who has looked upon her with favor as well. Her mentor's joyful welcome and sensitivity of soul create a safe and sacred space where Mary can sing her own song of praise for who she is and for what God is doing in her life.

If Mary is to sing, however, Elizabeth must keep silent.

Many potentially fruitful pastoral mentoring relationships flounder because the pastoral mentor will not shut up. The ego boost offered

5. Ibid.
6. Luke 1:46.

by assuming the pose of a ministry expert or pastoral super-hero before a supposedly star-struck student or staff member proves too irresistible. So the mentor takes center stage and drones on and on about his or her own stories, experiences, and life lessons, while the mentee sits passively as captive congregation to an un-asked-for sermon.

Sometimes mentors fall into the trap of talking too much because pastoral ministry can be a lonely vocation, and mentors find few places where someone seems actually willing to listen to them, rather than vice versa. Perhaps the pastor feels un-appreciated or un-noticed, and now, finally, his or her ministry has an audience! And yet while friendship can become a part of a mentoring relationship, no mentor should look to a protégé as the solution to his or her loneliness or need for affirmation. Mentees should never be used.[7]

Elizabeth was no doubt lonely herself. Luke relates that, prior to Mary's visit, Elizabeth had lived for five months in seclusion. She has had no one with whom she can talk. And yet after welcoming Mary into her home Elizabeth doesn't let her own neediness cause her to latch onto Mary the way a drowning woman reaches for a life-preserver. She assumes the posture of a listener. There will come a time when she can relate to Mary some of what she has learned about the experience of pregnancy—but first she keeps a silent space in which Mary can sing from her soul.

Parker Palmer, a Quaker writer and educator, has written that the soul is like a wild animal. Like a wild animal, "the soul is tough, resilient, resourceful, savvy, and self-sufficient: it knows how to survive in hard places." "Yet," Palmer continues,

> despite its toughness, the soul is also shy. Just like a wild animal, it seeks safety in the dense underbrush, especially when other people are around. If we want to see a wild animal, we know that the last thing we should do is go crashing through the woods yelling for it to come out. But if we will walk quietly into the woods, sit patiently at the base of the tree, breathe with the earth, and fade into our surroundings, the wild creature we seek might put in an appearance.[8]

7. Care should be taken that neither side in a mentoring relationship develops such an unhealthy attachment to the other. Especially until the relationship evolves into something more resembling friendship, respect for the boundaries of personhood are as important in mentoring relationships as in counseling ones—particularly with persons of the opposite sex.

8. Palmer, *Hidden Wholeness*, 58–59.

The best mentors are patient listeners. They do not go crashing into the woods of their mentee's life. They do not try to force or coerce a mentee into a greater degree of honesty or vulnerability. They do not rush in to solve the learner's problems for them. They do not too quickly offer advice and say, "This is what I would do." They do not try to "fix" what is broken in their protégé. They do not smother displays of genuine emotion as inappropriate. To do any of these things merely drives the student's soul more deeply into hiding in the underbrush.

The best mentors offer invitations instead of issuing demands or even suggestions, and then sit in trusting silence and wait for the soul to make its appearance, should it decide to reveal itself. They ask open and honest questions, questions they sincerely do not know the answer to, instead of "leading the witness" by camouflaging hidden instructions with a question mark. They listen from a deep conviction that God can be trusted to help a mentee to sort through their own struggles, that the student has, in Vanier's words, "the capacity to grow." Good mentors listen, and listen, and listen, and wait and wait and wait for as long as possible for the conversation to unspool before they jump in to offer counsel. When they do speak, they are willing to make themselves vulnerable by honestly relating some of their own mistakes and struggles and insecurities.

In doing so, the best mentors demonstrate a profound respect for the sacredness of another's freedom. They also reflect their faith in the presence of a third person, the Holy Spirit, in their midst. A good mentor cares deeply for the well-being of a mentee and yet at the same time holds the space between them, respects the borders of personhood, leaves room for the Holy Spirit. He or she allows their protégé to fail, to make mistakes, to hold different theological views, and to follow their own unique path rather than compelling the learner to follow one blazed by the mentor.

It is not only Elizabeth's welcome, but her silence, that leaves room for Mary to sing. Mary does of course take up some of her mentor's language into her song, singing of how all generations (and not just Elizabeth) will call her "blessed." Already an act of conscious or unconscious imitation is taking place on the part of the mentee. And yet the melody is Mary's own. Elizabeth doesn't interrupt, or even make the performance a duet.[9] She cedes the microphone to the *theotokos*.

9. At a revival I attended while writing this chapter, a young woman offered a moving testimony of how God had carried her through a period of deep grief after the loss of her husband, and then she sang a beautiful song of praise that deeply touched everyone present. It was a holy, transcendent moment. Suddenly, however, the male song leader

## ELIZABETH AND MENTORING WOMEN FOR MINISTRY

The example of how Elizabeth helps Mary to find her voice and claim her calling highlights the need for wise mentoring of women who are entering pastoral ministry. God gives to Mary the gift of a mentor of her own gender whom she can emulate, a colleague who understands her experience in a way no man ever fully could. Women entering pastoral ministry similarly need female mentors and role models who have an intimate knowledge of gender-specific realities of ministry. And yet in a church that is still over-whelmingly male in its leadership, the responsibility for offering faithful mentoring to female clergy rests upon both women and men.

Male and female clergy who are mentoring female students or colleagues can learn a lot from Elizabeth, particularly in her ability to create a space where Mary can be empowered to find her own voice. Some women who enter the pastorate grew up in Christian traditions where female voices are not included in or valued by leadership. Some have been taught (explicitly or implicitly) to be submissive or silent in the presence of a male authority figure. Even women who have not been raised in such backgrounds have occasionally imbibed sexist cultural messages that praise assertive male leaders as "strong and decisive" while demeaning assertive women. One female divinity student reflected upon the ways that these messages can serve as "vice grips" that hold back women and constrict pastoral mentoring relationships:

> These vice grips tell women that they should be gracious, submissive to men in leadership, not too forward, not too pushy, and not too sure of themselves because it makes men feel emasculated. They shouldn't dominate conversation because "everyone knows" that women talk too much. They shouldn't burden men with their emotional issues, (because) everyone knows it's just female hormones and not really important: give it a week and they will go away on their own. The cumulative effect of these attitudes creates barriers between the Male mentor and the Female men-tee . . . These dynamics are bubbling under the surface, and unless they are named they remain hidden but powerful.[10]

---

for the event (who seemed to really enjoy being in the "in front" position) picked up his microphone and joined in the song, and his deep and loud voice drowned out that of the young woman, much to our common chagrin. His action seemed a parable about mentoring, and represented the opposite of what Elizabeth does for Mary.

10. This quotation is taken from an email correspondence with a student at Duke Divinity School. Used with permission.

Some young women clergy additionally describe being condescended to by older male mentors and parishioners who treat them as a "pretty young thing" or who make jokes about ditzy blondes or nagging wives. They are forced to listen to comments related to their clothing or appearance far more often than their male colleagues. Another female pastor summarizes what she has learned about views towards women in positions of church leadership: "We've come a long way, baby, but we ain't there yet. Do not assume that because women have been 'allowed' in the pulpit for decades that they are always fully accepted there now."[11]

A good mentor to a female clergyperson (male or female) will recognize these dynamics faced by women in pastoral ministry and will respond with sensitivity. Like Elizabeth, the mentor will name Mary as blessed and called by God, and make space for her own voice to sing—and to be heard. A male mentor might also direct the female mentee to a trusted female colleague who could serve as a confidante, or the two might read a book together written about the experience of a woman in ministry. The mentor can offer empathy, a listening ear, and perhaps when appropriate, humor: as when mentor and mentee learn to shake their heads and laugh together at the crazy things church folks can say. The good mentor will also model appropriate behavior towards the female student or intern or staff member by acknowledging her authority, introducing her with the appropriate professional title, challenging sexist comments or behavior, and helping the congregation to imagine what it might be like to be a woman in ministry.

If the mentor is male, he might discover that this experience of walking with a female protégé opens his eyes to the prevalence of inequality in our world and in the church, and perhaps even to the depths of his own unconscious inherited sexism. It will, in short, make him a more faithful, perceptive, compassionate, and complete Christian.

## WHAT TO EXPECT WHEN YOU'RE EXPECTING

And Mary remained with her about three months and then returned to her home. Now the time came for Elizabeth to give birth, and she bore a son.

LUKE 1:56–57

11. This quotation is taken from an email correspondence with a female pastoral colleague. Used with permission.

Mary's relationship with Elizabeth doesn't end with the last strains of the Magnificat. Luke tells us that she remained with her mentor for about three months, serving in a kind of twelve-week rural field education internship in the practice of pregnancy.

No doubt Mary's presence was a great gift to her mentor after Elizabeth's five months of seclusion and silence. Mary's youth and energy animate the elder woman. Her questions challenge her to think more deeply about things she has too long taken for granted. Plus there is the help Mary can offer with the daily chores of the household.

For her part Mary talks with Elizabeth about the changes taking place within her—about the swollen ankles, the morning sickness, the strange cravings. Elizabeth mostly reassures her that what she is experiencing is normal, and that she is not crazy.

Mary receives not only the gift of Elizabeth's encouragement but also the gift of her example. She has the opportunity to watch how a righteous older woman lives her life, interacts with her husband, and loves her neighbors.[12] For three months, Elizabeth is able to serve as model and coach to Mary.

Mentoring involves not only the development of soul, but the instruction and acquisition of concrete skills, the honing of physical practice. Good pastoral mentors communicate the tricks of the trade, the secrets of the craft. They share with their apprentices the detailed "hows" and the "whys": the insights that guide them in how they plan for the week, lead worship, prepare sermons, offer a prayer, make a sick visit, respond to a request for financial assistance, conduct a meeting, or approach a conflict.

Good pastoral mentors not only communicate the principles of practice, but provide opportunities for practice itself that are accompanied by helpful non-intrusive coaching. Kenda Creasy Dean and Ron Foster have proposed a simple partnership teaching model for empowering young people for ministry that a mentor can adapt and use to help a mentee grow in a particular pastoral skill: 1. I do it, you watch. 2. I do it, you help. 3. You do it, I help. 4. You do it, I watch. 5. You do it, I move on to something else.[13]

Whether or not such a formal process was followed, Mary will learn a great deal from watching Elizabeth: she learns what to expect when you

12. One of the gifts a mentor offers to a learner is the opportunity to look over the shoulder of his or her life.

13. Dean and Foster, *God-Bearing Life*, 96. Kenda Creasy Dean and Ronald Foster's book offers a beautiful extended meditation on the image of the "God-bearer" as it relates to the Christian life.

are expecting. Perhaps Mary even learns how to give birth to a child. Luke tells us that Mary travels to visit Elizabeth at the close of the older woman's second trimester, and that she will remain with her for three months. This might mean that Mary is present with her mentor through baby John's birth.

If so, then Mary is there when the first contraction comes. She hears Elizabeth describe how it feels. She learns what it looks like when the water breaks. She takes in how to breathe, learns how to try to manage the pain, observes how to push at the right moment. She beholds the miracle of new life entering the world. Then for a few days Mary will learn how to care for this new life: how to hold the infant, how to swaddle him, how to help him to latch, how to burp him, how to soothe him with a coo or a song.

## FROM MENTOR TO MANGER TO MESSIAH

While they were there [in Bethlehem], the time came for [Mary] to deliver her child. And she gave birth to her firstborn son and wrapped him in bands of cloth, and laid him in a manger, because there was no place for them in the inn.

LUKE 2:6–7

By the time Mary returns to her home in Nazareth, she is a different person. She is ready.

Six months later, in the little town of Bethlehem, alone and away from family, when the worst contractions come, Mary thinks of Elizabeth.

When little Jesus is born, and Mary wraps him in swaddling clothes, her husband marvels at the strength she has shown, beholds how natural Mary is with the child, wonders where she ever could have learned such a thing.

But it's no mystery. It's a mentor.

Elizabeth has shown Mary how to welcome new life into this world.

Now Mary will get to become a kind of mentor herself. She will mother another *theotokos* who has the life of God within him, nurture another to follow God's outrageous call.

She truly is blessed.

## BIBLIOGRAPHY

Bonhoeffer, Dietrich. *Life Together; Prayerbook of Bible*. Edited by Geffrey B. Kelly. Translated by Daniel W. Bloesch and James H. Burtness. Dietrich Bonhoeffer Works 5. Minneapolis: Fortress, 1996.

Dean, Kenda Creasy, and Ron Foster. *God-Bearing Life: Art of Soul Tending for Youth Ministry*. Nashville: Upper Room, 1998.

Nouwen, Henri J. M. *Genesee Diary: Report from Trappist Monastery*. New York: Doubleday, 1976.

Palmer, Parker J. *Hidden Wholeness: Journey Toward an Undivided Life*. San Francisco: Jossey-Bass/John Wiley, 2004.

Vanier, Jean. *Broken Body: Journey to Wholeness*. London: Darton, Longman, and Todd, 1988.

# Chapter 2

# Lucky, and Promiscuous

## James C. Howell

A MEMORABLE AHA! MOMENT for me came in seminary when I heard Professor David Steinmetz tell us about John Staupitz, Luther's superior in the Augustinian Order. As Steinmetz explained in his book, *Luther and Staupitz*, "Staupitz took an interest in this retiring, bookish young man who bombarded him in the confessional with trivial faults inflated by his scrupulous imagination into what he feared were mortal sins. Staupitz gave him absolution for his real sins, subjected him to a cold but bracing shower of sound theology and common sense, and groomed him to be his own replacement."[1]

Luther had a mentor. That someone in the pantheon of historical geniuses might have had a mentor had never dawned on me. I suppose I assumed that a genius simply burst onto the scene, a novum out of nowhere. The hackneyed, corny saying, "Behind every great man, there's a great woman" (and now the droll "Behind every great man, there's a woman rolling her eyes"), must hold some truth. All of us are great debtors to someone, to many someones. The Cappadocians Basil and Gregory likely would be unknown to us were it not for the mentoring of their big sister Macrina; she accused her baby brother Basil of being puffed up, and she was the one

---

1. Steinmetz, *Luther and Staupitz*, 8–9.

who first blazed their trail to renunciation and the monastic life. Francis of Assisi asked the priest (whose name we regrettably don't know) at San Damiano for guidance. Martin Luther King learned from Reinhold Niebuhr, and relied on Mahalia Jackson to sing to him to lift his sagging spirits.

I got lucky the day I started seminary. I literally bumped into a tall, gangly gentleman with white hair and the kind of roaring voice we associate with God: Father Roland Murphy,[2] distinguished Old Testament scholar, Carmelite priest, an unforgettable teacher—and eventually my mentor. I don't recall ever asking, "Will you be my mentor?" It just happened, or maybe God orchestrated it all; or more likely he was the kind of professor who took an interest in young people, and had cultivated sufficient wisdom and tender care in his own soul as to be of enough value to them that they kept coming back to him. I found him to be extremely busy and yet always available. His door was rarely shut, and however absorbed he might be clacking away at his typewriter with German tomes sprawled across his desk, he would always stop and give me as much time as I needed. The grace of availability; the surprise of interruptibility; the mercy of time granted.

I took every class he offered, and pestered him more than a student should. I was his research assistant, and he directed my doctoral dissertation. But more importantly, he was sage, friend, counselor, guide, and mentor. Father Murphy was like a father to me. I never made an important life decision without consulting with him. As the years passed, he made a point of getting together with me for lunch or dinner, even when it was probably inconvenient for him. Small talk bored him, so he would cut to the chase and speak of things that mattered, probing deeply, reflecting wisely.

Sometimes a single word from him would perform some kind of surgery on my heart. In one of our last conversations, I was reporting to him how much I loved the church I was serving, how swimmingly well things were going, how lovely a setting it was for me to live out a fulfilling ministry and family life. With no hint of chiding, he asked, "But do you ever worry about getting complacent in such a fine place?" *Complacent.* The word kept intruding into my consciousness, haunting me, like the very voice of some ancient prophet, or even that of the Lord God Almighty.

He died, with considerable panache, the day after his eighty fifth birthday, on what Roman Catholics observe as the Feast Day of Elijah—not bad for a professor of Old Testament who belonged to the Carmelite Order! Like all good mentors, Roland's life wasn't about himself, but about

---

2. Howell, "Heroes Found Faithful."

the material he taught, the "others," always, and the order of God's church. I know I did not thank him nearly enough. Yes, I tendered thank you notes, a festschrift contribution, a book dedication and other gestures. Perhaps he overheard my affectionate remarks at his memorial service. Most likely, the best thanks a mentor can receive would be a ministry well-pursued and a life well-lived.

One piece of his counsel was that in the first half of your life you labor hard to succeed, to become somebody; then in the second half of your life you do all you can to help others succeed and become somebody. I've tried to take that as seriously as possible. My greatest pleasure in my professional life has been the cultivation of relationships with others who need a listening ear, some attentiveness, a little encouragement. How lucky I am that a handful of mostly younger clergy have taken their time to share their lives with me, to explore the confusions and complexities of ministry together, to prayerfully engage with me in learning and growing together. I'm the beneficiary, and have learned so much from them.

But I'm entirely clear on this: it isn't the case that I had a mentor, and then after that I become one. I desperately needed mentoring back then— and now. Father Murphy died in 2002, and I have missed him terribly. Since losing him, I've tried to fill in that gap—and the way I have done so helps me realize that even during his lifetime I had multiple mentors. I know I do now.

Of course, it is an immeasurable blessing to have a mentor, one person you can name with whom you've built trust, where despite the evident identities of mentor and mentee there really is reciprocity, and a long term, regular relationship. Others in this volume have written well on how to be the mentor, and what to look for in the mentor. When I find myself in that role, I commit myself to check in regularly, to shoot a little text or hand-written note near perilous moments, and to listen and dabble in leading questions more than spouting any wisdom I might think I have. Sometimes you just don't have *a* mentor—but mentoring can still happen.

When it comes to corralling wisdom and direction, I am a bit promiscuous. I'll take it from any and everybody, and I'm never ashamed to ask. Maybe you never get as lucky as I was to have a Father Murphy. But there can be a crowd of mentors, and getting what you need might feel like the way William Faulkner said you might write a novel: it's like building a chicken coop in high wind; you grab any board or shingle flying by or loose on the ground and nail it down fast.[3] My first month in ministry I bumped into an older clergyman as we entered the hospital to visit. Bypassing the elevator, he opened the door to the stairwell and said, "Always take the stairs." And I always have, and take some pride in being slightly more fit in my sedentary profession because I got mentored, however briefly, that day.

And so I have constantly placed phone calls, emails and now texts to clergy, professors, and a smorgasbord of others, asking unabashedly how to handle a pericope or a personnel quandary, what to do with a recalcitrant musician, or how to explain apophaticism to laity. My debts are too numerous to count or begin to repay. I think my short attention span makes me a candidate for this kind of profligate tendency to get and grab little bits of mentoring where I can. The relationship I had with Fr. Murphy was clearly richer and far more significant. But if your best friend or spouse died, you'd be grateful for a burger and a beer at lunch with somebody, anybody.

We may ponder the curious way God works when it comes to mentoring. Much of the time, probably most of the time, the one who has a big impact on you just has no idea what she said mattered or was even heard. Or you try to be of support to someone, and there's no evidence it "took"—but then in God's mercy your wisdom resurfaces, perhaps unrecognized, and provides genuine help. As Charles Williams put it, "The altar must often be built in one place so that the fire may come down in another place."[4]

How the fire comes down surprises in another way. When I was in seminary, I drew a summer assignment where I was to be mentored by a clergy person who, unbeknownst to me or the seminary, was teetering on the precipice of burnout. He wasn't much interested or really able to mentor me, so dense was his own darkness. And yet we wound up spending hours in deep conversation that probably did more for my ministerial and personal development than any interactions I'd had with a chipper, well-intentioned supervisor. His exposure of his brokenness, and the brutal questions he grappled with in front of me transformed me, humbled me, nudged me toward an earthier kind of theology.

And then sometimes you wonder if you are part of God's broader drama in which grace happens certainly but indirectly. I am a curious mixture of success and failure, in mentoring, in being mentored, and in my private life—and so I find myself very attached to a remark Margaret Miles made in her wonderful *Augustine and the Fundamentalist's Daughter*: "I feel anguish

---

3. Peterson, *Under the Unpredictable Plant*, 6.

4. As quoted by C. S. Lewis in his final interview. See Wirt, "Final Interview."

over my inability to help my son, and suffer from the irony that I have spent my life teaching other people's children. But I can help others' children, and so I do. And I hope that, in the broader generosity of the universe, there will be someone who can help my son."[5]

The longtime president of Harvard, Charles William Eliot, famously said that "books are the quietest and most constant of friends; they are the most accessible and wisest of counselors, and the most patient of teachers."[6] And my finest mentors. It is entirely true when I say that over many years I have developed intimate relationships with Dorothy Day, Hans Urs von Balthasar, Howard Thurman, Rowan Williams, Evelyn Underhill, and quite a few others whose books line my library shelves; I never met any of them, but we're quite close.

I was similarly attached to Elie Wiesel, Eugene Peterson, Walter Brueggemann, Jürgen Moltmann, and Barbara Brown Taylor—and was lucky enough to meet them long after the relationship (on my end) had blossomed. When we did meet, I tried not to stammer, gawk, or ask for a selfie, but it was difficult, so immense was my debt to such giants. How many hours and how much emotion did I invest reading Karl Barth's *Church Dogmatics* (and his other books)? Even the most generous living human being could never allow me so much time. Augustine, Luther, Thérèse, Teresa, Gregory, Gregory and Gregory, Julian, a holy cloud of witnesses, all of whom I count as my wisest and constantly available mentors.

And so when I think of these mentors who have helped me to hear God, I resonate easily to Thomas Merton's thought: "Reading ought to be an act of homage to the God of all truth. We open our hearts to words that reflect the reality He has created or the greater Reality which He is. It is also an act of humility and reverence towards other men who are the instruments by which God communicated His truth to us. Reading gives God more glory when we get more out of it, when it is a more deeply vital act not only of our intelligence but of our whole personality, absorbed and refreshed . . . Books can speak to us like God."[7]

Authors of books have mentored me in ministry and life—and not just the blatantly religious writers. While books on ministerial leadership leave me cold, I'm only a little less bored by their secular counterparts, and yet have benefited some from Edwin Friedman, Ron Heifetz and Patrick

---

5. Miles, *Augustine and the Fundamentalist's Daughter*, 95.

6. Eliot, "Happy Life," 37.

7. Merton, *Thoughts in Solitude*, 62.

Lencioni. I've found that, when it comes to business, there is no substitute for simply finding a successful small business owner in your town or congregation and asking "How do you do it?"

What I've learned from historians and biographers (like David Halberstam or Taylor Branch or Doris Kearns Goodwin) about lives well lived and movements that flourish have inspired and instructed me. Poets (from Homer to Mary Oliver) have patiently taught me to be careful with words and emotions. Oddly, the greatest learning may have come, for me, at the feet of writers of fiction. I like the idea that, in heaven, you will be able to converse, not only with grandparents and saints from the past, but even fictional characters. Some have actually been exemplary preachers, like Dilsey's preacher in *The Sound and the Fury*, the mesmerizing Dinah Morris in *Adam Bede*, and even Father Tim of the *Mitford* novels. There are laity too: Jayber Crow, Atticus Finch, Frodo, and of course Owen Meany. Buffoons, in fiction (Elmer Gantry?) and in real life (no need to use names here) can function as anti-mentors: you see it done badly, which is precisely what impels you to re-envision how to do it better. Isaac Watts wrote his best hymns after he complained about the dull music in church; his father replied, "Well then, young man, why don't you give us something better to sing?"

Finally, and perhaps most importantly, as I grow older I realize the most valuable mentors I have had and shall ever have are the young. At his inauguration in October, 1978, Pope John Paul II spoke not to the masses so much as to the young, reaching out to them by saying "You are the hope of the Church and of the world. You are my hope." I have known young clergy who might say I was mentoring them. But really the privilege was mine to sit with them, toss questions and ideas around, and hear their perspectives. The young have that fledgling fire, that unjaded zeal that can blow my old, smoldering embers back to life. The millennials can cockily believe they already know how to do all things well—which can be annoying, but then again, they aren't so far wrong a lot of the time.

Perhaps I have stretched the definition of "mentor" beyond any reasonable limit. But I'll count on the elasticity, and as I take the stairs, carrying a book or two, I'll text somebody with a question, and smile broadly, knowing mentoring is going on all around. Roland Murphy lives on, in my grateful memory, and hopefully in the ministries of students he never met. God's goodness, which for me feels like blessed luck, is unbounded.

# BIBLIOGRAPHY

Eliot, Charles W. "The Happy Life." In *The Durable Satisfactions of Life.* New York: T. Y. Crowell, 1910, reprinted 2015.

Howell, James C. "Heroes Found Faithful: Father Roland E. Murphy." http://heroesfoundfaithful.blogspot.com/2010/11/father-roland-e-murphy.html.

Merton, Thomas. *Thoughts in Solitude.* New York: Noonday, 1956.

Miles, Margaret. *Augustine and the Fundamentalist's Daughter.* Eugene, OR: Cascade, 2011.

Peterson, Eugene H. *The Contemplative Pastor: Returning to the Art of Spiritual Direction.* Grand Rapids: Eerdmans, 1993.

———. *Under the Unpredictable Plant: An Exploration in Vocational Holiness.* Grand Rapids: Eerdmans, 1992.

Steinmetz, David. *Luther and Staupitz: Essay in Intellectual Origins of Protestant Reformation.* Durham: Duke University Press, 1980.

Wirt, Sherwood Eliot. "The Final Interview of C. S. Lewis." *Decision*, September 1963.

# *Chapter 3*

# Three Practices

## ELAINE HEATH

"NEVER TEACH DOCTRINE TO a new believer," my mentor, Reverend Betty Jeavons, repeated. "Instead, teach them to gaze at the One who gazes at them with infinite love. Teach them to pray gazing prayer. If you will teach a new believer to pray in this way, grounded in their belovedness to God, they will come to recognize good doctrine, and they will become people who truly love and follow Jesus. You want to help them feel at home with God, able to rest in God's presence. That is much more important than doctrine. Get them grounded in love, then you can move into doctrine." She went on to describe how early indoctrination deforms new Christians into uptight legalists who think that Christianity is essentially about intellectual propositions, and who become hardened to the internal movement of the Spirit that goes deeper than arguments and words.

I myself at that time was a young adult who was enamored of doctrine and generally lived in my head. I was a committed dualistic thinker, as Richard Rohr would put it. I nodded as if in agreement, though what she said did not make me happy. Not only did her words diminish the ultimate value I wanted to place upon correct doctrine, teaching others "gazing prayer" would require me to pray that way myself, which would require me to get out of my head and into the misty realms of the heart, territory best left to others. I wondered how it would be to gaze at the One who gazes at me with infinite love. I wondered if I was able. I wondered if Betty knew how uncertain I felt. I wondered why she trusted me so much. I wondered if she would still love me if I disappointed her.

Betty loved me no matter what, but it took a long time before I understood that. And I was much more transparent than I knew. All my questions and uncertainties were written plainly on my face, yet Betty was gracious, always treating me with kindness and respect.

The context for our conversation was a women's group that I had begun leading under Betty's supervision. There were about thirty women and I was teaching them the basics of Christian discipleship. Each week I spent hours preparing for the upcoming two-hour session with its gathering worship, teaching, small group processing time, prayer, and pastoral care of the women involved. I spent hours because I wanted to be sure all my doctrinal bases were covered. Leading such a group was a new experience for me and I desperately wanted to get it right. Often I sat with Betty over a cup of coffee, fretting and debriefing, gradually relaxing as she listened and responded in her gentle, perceptive way.

Betty had asked me to lead the group—one she had founded several years earlier—after I participated in it for several months. To my astonishment one summer day she said, "I am wondering if you would lead the Tuesday group this coming year? I'm in need of some rest. Mary Anne will help you." I blinked mutely, wondering how in the world I could teach this group when I was young, inexperienced, nervous, and a complete beginner. After a few stammered attempts to decline her offer, it became clear that she would not be deterred. "Mary Anne will help you," she repeated mildly for the third time, meaning that our mutual friend would take care of hospitality issues so that I could focus on teaching and leading.

So it was that Reverend Betty Jeavons, who had begun companioning me two years earlier, gradually guided me into a ministry context so that I could experience God's call. She did not refer to herself as mentor, nor did we label our relationship as anything except friends. Yet she was a superb mentor, the most impactful one of my life. I am unable to imagine mentoring the many young adults I companion today, without drawing from Betty's wisdom and method.

The three most important practices I learned from Betty, which I now use in mentoring others, are:

1. For in-depth mentoring find multiple ways to build genuine friend-ship where you "do life" together in community.

2. Provide opportunities for the mentee to work with you as an appren-tice, and in that context call forth, affirm, and empower the gifts of the mentee.

3. Cultivate the spiritual life of the mentee through example and shared theological reflection.

These three practices are needed in varying degrees depending upon the mentee and the situation. The first practice incorporates the other two and is only for certain kinds of mentees, as I will explain. The other two practices are essential for mentoring persons into leaders who lead as disciples.

## LIFE TOGETHER

True friendship requires mutuality, vulnerability, trust, and shared expe-riences. Much time is needed for this kind of friendship to deepen and mature. The cultivation of lifelong, spiritual friendship with a mentee is not required for every mentoring relationship, but is absolutely necessary for some. I think of these as "Elijah and Elisha" relationships, where there must be much more engagement than a sharing of wisdom and guidance of an individual toward some aspect of vocation. In this case the mentoring has to do with companioning the mentee into full recognition and acceptance of her or his identity and entire vocation, and often involves healing of old wounds that hinder the mentees' capacity to live into their vocation. This kind of relationship evolves over the years from a mentoring friendship into a mutual friendship of peers.

In seminary future ministers and theologians learn that clear profes-sional boundaries are necessary at all times with every person with whom they work, including colleagues and subordinates. Students are taught not to expect or cultivate friendship with future subordinates, congregants, or anyone else with whom they have a professional role. "Never make friends with parishioners!" they are warned. They are urged to find professional peers outside of their immediate context with whom to develop safe and trusting relationships, but in fact such relationships become very difficult because of the competitive climate in which clergy and theologians work. There is also the possibility that today's clergy friend may be tomorrow's bishop who has authority over you, so you must be careful what you share even with trusted colleagues. In this setting it becomes nearly impossible to cultivate an "Elijah-Elisha" mentoring friendship.

The modern emphasis on strict professional boundaries is meant to protect institutions and their employees from lawsuits, frankly, and generally awkward situations. It is part of our overwhelmingly risk-averse society. I often wonder, though, what Jesus and Paul would make of these rules.

Jesus lived and traveled with his primary mentees—both women[1] and men—and in the process of being in community, showed them how to live into their vocation. It was very messy and at times a disaster. There were fights, people jockeying for position, misunderstandings, and chronic weariness. Jesus, who was accused by detractors of being a drunk and glutton because of all that libatious friendship, developed deep and lasting relationships with his motley crew. His action-reflection pedagogy was thoroughly contextualized in countless shared meals, the inconvenient lack of resources while in mission, opposition from authorities, and sick people. Every encounter, whether pigs, storms, or lepers, provided an opportunity for mentoring in real life. There were no classes, no books to read other than Scripture, no tests and no papers. There was only the school of life together.

Deep mentoring in the way of Jesus requires doing life together. In the process of life, with all its ups and downs, old wounds surface. Bigotries rear their ugly heads. Petty grievances, jealousies, insecurities, and ambitions all come to the table. So do gifts, graces, talents, insights. Vocation emerges. Doing life together provides the best possible environment for a mentee to learn to do their inner work as well as their outer work so that they can live into their God-given identity and vocation with integrity.

The Apostle Paul, like Jesus, formed deep, family-like friendships with those whom he mentored most closely. His language would appall contemporary shapers of professional boundaries in seminaries: "We could have thrown our weight around as Christ's apostles. Instead, we were gentle with you like a nursing mother caring for her own children. We were glad to share not only God's good news with you but also our very lives because we cared for you so much. You remember, brothers and sisters, our efforts and hard work. We preached God's good news to you, while we worked night and day so we wouldn't be a burden on any of you" (1 Thess 2:7–9).

---

1. Luke 8:1–3 CEB.

Elsewhere Paul describes his young mentee, Timothy, as his "true child in the faith" (1 Tim 1:1–2). We do not know precisely how much time Paul spent with Timothy, but it is clear that their relationship was deep and trusting, covering much more territory than simply the exchange of information as to how to lead a church. We also know that Timothy's father was not a Christian and that chronic illness and anxiety were significant challenges to him in his ministry. Paul's investment of himself in Timothy provided the holistic grounding Timothy needed for faithful service.

One of the first things that Betty did to welcome me into her life was to invite me to eat a meal with her. Over subsequent shared meals and unhurried conversation, friendship blossomed. Our families gradually became friends, getting together for birthdays, holidays and other occasions. We became available to help each other during times of illness or other need. Our communities of friends began to mingle and in some cases overlap.

Though Betty was far more mature than I, and old enough to be my mother, she always referred to me as her friend and she treated me respectfully and with honor as a friend. She resisted using maternal language about her role in my life, preferring instead the biblical nomenclature of "sister." Through genuine friendship Betty taught me valuable ministry and leadership concepts such as helping new Christians learn to pray before loading them up with doctrine. But more importantly she gave me herself. I could see her living her actual life as a deeply devoted follower of Jesus. Through hundreds of shared life experiences she imparted to me wisdom that continues to guide me today, decades later.

The degree to which we are able to share life in friendship with our mentees is determined by a number of factors including gender, age, our and their family dynamics, time available, and the kind of vocation for which we are mentoring another person. Healthy boundaries—the sort you keep with any healthy friendship—must be kept by the mentor and fostered in the mentee. With regard to boundaries in general, I abide by Paul's injunction to young Timothy in 1 Tim 5:2, treating those who are around my age as sisters or brothers, those younger as nieces or nephews, and those older as aunts or uncles, with familial affection and appropriate sexual boundaries. I regularly see a spiritual director who provides support and accountability for me in my work of mentoring, among other things. While the number of people I mentor to this degree is small, the impact of such mentoring is disproportionately impactful, reaching indirectly into the lives of many people and institutions. In my own life I doubt I could have heard my call or responded courageously and consistently for the rest of my life, had Betty not mentored me in this manner.

## APPRENTICESHIP AND CALLING FORTH GIFTS

Mentoring Christian leaders has everything to do with helping people live into their call. The reason a mentee seeks a mentor's guidance is usually that their call is something like the mentor's. It may not be exactly the same, but there are enough similarities that the mentee hopes the mentor will impart to them wisdom as well as practical skills with which to carry out their work. The most effective way to do this for a mentee is to provide opportunities for the mentee to work alongside you and experience your vocation with you. This apprenticeship approach is exactly how Jesus trained the approximately one hundred twenty persons who launched the church at Pentecost (Acts 1:12–15).

Jesus first invited followers to come and travel with him and watch as he ministered to people. As they watched they had plenty of questions and at times were offended by Jesus' actions. He ate with sinners, drank from a Samaritan woman's cup, broke Sabbath laws, and responded to critics. All of that was grist for the mill of learning. He acted, then reflected with them based upon their questions and concerns. Jesus was like a good Montessori teacher, shaping the lessons around the readiness of his mentees to learn. Their questions and their aversion were the pivot points for each learning situation. Along the way he increased their degree of involvement so that they moved from spectators to participants. The feeding of the five thousand is one example. "You feed them!" he said when they complained of people's hunger. So they did.

Gradually Jesus gave them opportunities to serve when he was not present. Luke 9:1–6 describes the first mission trip of the twelve who were Jesus' inner circle. He gave them authority and sent them out, admonishing them to simplicity and a spartan lifestyle while on the journey. They returned and he took them away for a time of debriefing.

Not long afterward Jesus sent out seventy or seventy two disciples in a similar manner with matching instructions. When he briskly ordered them to take no extra clothing, no money, no food, nothing but themselves and a willingness to humbly receive hospitality when it was offered, what he described to them was his own lifestyle. That was exactly how they had seen him live and had lived with him up to that point. But just to make things clear he spelled it out for them in a list of instructions. His method worked.

When Betty invited me to take over the group she had started years before, it was not because she was tired and needed a break! She saw that I needed to experience my God-given but as-of-yet unrecognized teaching and leadership gifts. She also wanted to be able to guide me along, help me correct course when I made mistakes, and protect me from potential political situations that are common to all churches. By handing her group over to me she was providing a laboratory for me to walk into my vocation. Wisely, she did not tell me what she was up to. After a year of leading the group and experiencing increasing inner freedom and outward fruit for my labor, I began to experience God's call in clear and repeated encounters. I saw that my vocation would include three distinct elements: pastoral ministry, academia, and a role in which I would resource the church at large in a way that would contribute to renewal. It all seemed too big and impossible, but the call was repeated and came from multiple sources. After a couple of weeks of these experiences I went to Betty and told her what was happening and how overwhelmed and frightened I felt. To my great surprise she threw back her head and laughed hard, joyfully telling me that she had seen it the day we met three years earlier, but never told me what she had seen because I would need to experience it all for myself. "You will not believe what God is going to do in your life," she said with quiet intensity. I stared in wonder as she wiped moisture from her eyes. She talked to me then about how I must always say "yes" to God's call. "If you will say 'yes,' God will make a way," she said. I promised her that I would do all in my power to say yes and keep saying yes. Betty never did tell me all that God had shown her about my future ministry. In retrospect, I believe God revealed glimpses of my future to her precisely so that she would devote the time and energy it took to mentor me.

In addition to inviting me to lead the group, Betty had begun to treat me like a trusted colleague, something I found unnerving. She began inviting me to go with her when she made hospital visits or home visits to encourage people who were suffering. She would ask me to pray with her and invite me to pray for her at times, rather than always praying for me. While planning to lead a retreat she would go over her plans and ask for my input. When she had a rough day or something challenging happened, Betty shared vulnerably with me. From time to time she recommended books for my edification, especially the work of Paul Tournier and Madame Guyon, but for the most part her way of calling forth my gifts was by inviting me to companion her in her work and then giving me opportunities to work with, then without her. Betty provided space and a context where I could, in Parker Palmer's terms, let my life speak.[2] Deep mentoring requires this kind of sustained involvement, presence, thoughtfulness, energy, and friendship.

## CULTIVATE A LIFE OF PRAYER

It is said that Evelyn Underhill[3] was finally brought to Christian faith not by the hundreds of books she read while researching Christian mysticism but by listening to her spiritual director pray. As a young adult, Underhill went to Baron Friedrich von Hügel for guidance. Disillusioned with Christianity and seeking a deeper understanding of the universal phenomenon of mysticism, she sought von Hügel's help because of his scholarly expertise in Christian mysticism and his reputation as a trustworthy spiritual director. After her conversion, Underhill went on to become the most widely read spiritual writer of the first half of the twentieth century. Several of her books are classics in Christian spirituality, continuing to shape the lives of Christians around the world. What called forth her real vocation as a spiritual leader was von Hügel's Jesus-like mentoring of her life of prayer.

As the disciples journeyed with Jesus they observed him pray in many different settings with different forms of prayer. Luke's Gospel most fully captures the breadth of Jesus' prayer practice as he mentored the future leaders of the church. The Lord's Prayer, given by Jesus to his disciples when they explicitly asked him to teach them to pray, summarizes Jesus' life. He was a living prayer. Above all else, Jesus taught his disciples to listen and be present to God, who was present to them. He helped them learn to trust the direction that is given in such prayer, and to lean into the belovedness that encircled them within the sacred community of the Trinity.[4] His final mentoring of them as he faced his own death, focused on the central fact of love. In the end, that was what mattered the most.

Today, many years later, I recall with deep gratitude the lesson I did not want to learn from Betty. "Teach them to gaze at the One who gazes at them with infinite love," she said. Her unspoken message was, "Elaine, gaze

2. Palmer, *Let Your Life Speak*. One of my favorite books on discernment of vocation.
3. http://www.evelynunderhill.org.
4. We find this teaching explicitly in Jesus' prayer in John 17.

at Jesus who gazes at you with infinite love. Live in that gaze and you will know how to live and what to believe."

As I recall the manner in which Betty mentored me, which has deeply shaped how I mentor others, what I remember more clearly than anything was how she prayed. There was such tenderness, such simplicity, such love. As I went through many difficult life circumstances Betty prayed with and for me. Over many years I learned to gaze at the One who gazes at me with infinite love. Like Friedrich von Hügel with Evelyn Underhill, the single most important aspect of Betty's mentoring was her prayer with and for me.

Over the past twenty years I have had numerous opportunities to mentor people to varying degrees, who are discovering and beginning to live into their call. For the past seven years I have been privileged to co-lead the Missional Wisdom Foundation, an organization that includes networks of intentional communities, missional faith communities, and other initiatives that provide laboratories for life together for the purpose of mentoring persons into their missional vocation. Nothing has given me greater joy than to companion persons as they discover God's gifts and call and begin to live faithfully in a Godward direction. This form of ministry would not be possible had I not received stellar mentoring as a young adult. Betty's mentoring prepared me for my vocation in ways neither of us could have fully known at the time. This is what outstanding mentoring does, both passing on the wisdom and something of the character of the mentor, and calling forth the unique gifts and vocation of the mentee.

## BIBLIOGRAPHY

Palmer, Parker J. *Let Your Life Speak: Listening for the Voice of Vocation.* San Francisco: Jossey-Bass, 1999.

*Chapter 4*

# As the Father Has Sent Me, So I Send You
## Mentoring in the Light of Jesus' Ascension

### SAMUEL WELLS

THERE'S A CLASSIC DREAM that almost everyone has. Schoolchildren have it: they're walking into an exam and they suddenly realize they've not been to classes for the last year. Actors have it: they're on stage and they completely blank on their lines. Executives have it: they're presenting to the board but they haven't a clue what the quarterly accounts are saying.

To be a mentor is to create a place of growth and discovery in which a person can learn, change, practice, and experiment. It is to enter the field of education. And as in all education, there's a lurking fear that someone's going to find out, publicly or privately, that you're a fraud, and you have no idea what you're talking about.

Our society isn't at all sure how to think about education. At one extreme is the rather naïve idea that education means simply drawing out of the boundless storehouse of each individual the wondrous depths that are there. At the other extreme is the rather soulless sense that the young mind is a blank slate and it's the teacher's job to transfer as much information onto it as possible before anyone notices. Between those two extremes lie two similar but subtly different notions. One is the idea of training—the learning of particular skills suited to adult life and the workplace, skills that equip the trainee to adapt to new circumstances with alacrity and confidence. The other is the idea of formation—the chiseling of character through resilient emergence from setback and disappointment to grow in wisdom and virtue.

All of these are part of the imagination and rhetoric of education to-day, even though sometimes they contradict one another; but my sense is that what draws people into teaching and inspires people to be mentors is something beyond all four of those notions. It's the image of giving a pupil or trainee a key that unlocks a whole universe, beyond and above and within and beneath the standard, everyday world they would otherwise perceive. It's just a glimpse of what the disciples felt around Jesus—that thrilling and irresistible sense that this is what life is, this is what the world is, this is what I am, this is who God is. To be a teacher or mentor is to be called to give people that key.

So how do you go about giving people that key? There are all sorts of theories and formulas, but what I find the simplest and the best goes like this.[1] You start with people who have low interest and low ability, not because they're bored or stupid but because they're new to the subject; your job is to direct them, to give them clear instructions and roles and tasks and vocabulary so they get a handle on what you're about. Then if all goes well you find you have people with high interest yet still low ability. They're into it, but still lack the tools and knowledge to put their interest to work. Your job is to coach them so they contribute their ideas and suggestions and to supervise them so through listening, advice, encouragement and example they can practice and get better at what they're doing. Then thirdly you find you have people who have high ability but maybe their interest is waning a little. The real work of the teacher here is to get inside people's motivations and build confidence through praise and persuasion. When someone looks back and credits a teacher for believing in them, this is the stage they're referring to. Finally, if all is well, you have people who have high interest and high ability, and they're ready to take up the reins and ideally grow into even greater knowledge and skill than their teacher; besides mentor-ing with decision-making and encouraging reflective practice, the teacher's main job is to let the baby eagle leave the nest and fly.

Directing, coaching, supporting and delegating: they're often thought of as forms of good management, but I see them as the shape of good teach-ing and mentoring. If you think about the people who were or are your best

1. Hersey and Blanchard, *Management of Organizational Behavior.*

33

teachers or mentors, the chances are they were with you in all four of these ways. If you've known what it feels like to be thrown in the deep end too quickly and set up to fail then you've been propelled into stage four without anyone helping you sufficiently with stages one, two, and three. If you've ever got cross with someone because you feel you've given them instructions and they've not done what you wanted them to do, maybe you've concentrated on stages one and four and neglected the coaching and support that are the vital way to get from one to the other.

In case this all seems a bit formulaic, think about Jesus' practice as a teacher. At the start of the gospels he does a lot of directing. He offers the Beatitudes, he describes the kingdom of God, he teaches in parables, he heals people as tangible signs of heaven on earth. The confused and foolish disciples start to get the message. Then he starts to do a bit more coaching. He sends the disciples out on mission trips. He equips them and advises them and debriefs them afterwards. Then for example in his long address at the Last Supper in John's gospel he does quite a bit of supporting. He anticipates a time when he will no longer be with them and talks more intensely about what it will mean for them to be clothed with the Spirit and given power to do the things he has been doing. Finally on Ascension Day he delegates: he steps aside, or in his case, he steps above, and he leaves the disciples to carry on the embodiment and proclamation of the gospel. Of course he promises, through the Holy Spirit, to be always available for guidance, strength, and encouragement, after he himself has returned to the Father. Jesus is the perfect teacher. He gives his disciples the keys to the kingdom, enabling them to discover through him what the world is, what life is, who they are and who God is. He directs, coaches, supports, and delegates. He has the words of eternal life.

Let me suggest how this may be embodied in pastoral ministry. A new, junior pastor joins the clergy team straight from seminary. They are at the base of the learning curve: they don't know what they don't know. But perhaps they have a strong desire to express themselves in front of a congregation, and a sense that they are joining a congregation that needs some fresh blood to shake things up. How might their senior pastor prepare them to lead worship appropriately, reverently, and engagingly?

- Directing. For the first Sunday or two the message is, "This is how we do it."

◊ That means getting the thinking right. The pastor has three roles: to speak to God for the people, for example in the pastoral prayer or prayers of the people; to speak to the people for God, for example in the sermon or in pronouncing blessing or absolving sins; and to help the people better to speak to one another, for example in the announcements. The mentor ensures the new pastor can tell the difference between the three, and speak in different ways depending on what is being done.

◊ It means getting the enactment right, with voice, movement, and choice of words. Some of this is simple rehearsal (after we share the peace we move to the table); some of it is human understanding (you can't absolve sins unless you are looking with compassion on the people you're talking to); some of it is rigorous attention to detail (what do you think you're communicating if when you do the announcements you speak anxiously, without the right level of detail and without connecting them to the church's faith and mission?).

◊ It means getting the basics memorized and internalized so there is room for spontaneity when the unexpected happens. The most telling things in liturgy are how people respond when a person faints or the communion chalice is dropped and spills or a lector trips and falls. A new pastor needs to gain such a deep understanding of the spirit of the occasion that they can respond appropriately when something that might seem embarrassing can quickly become a door to deeper encounter.

◊ There's no substitute for walking together through the sanctuary and practicing words and actions until they become second nature.

• Coaching. The key words here are listening, advice, encouragement and example.

◊ The observations of a newcomer are a precious gift. This isn't how we do it at my church. Why on earth do you sing a hymn straight after the sermon? If you place your hands over the bread and cup when you say the words of institution, what do you do with your hands when you invoke the Spirit on the congregation? Such reflections can be challenges to deeper understanding, clearer expression, transformed practice. A two-way learning emerges as the trainee begins to discover what they don't know and evaluate what they do know.

◊ The mentor can balance the coaching given before the event and the feedback given after. In my experience coaching is more valuable than feedback. Feedback can explore what went wrong and why and how to improve things for next time; good coaching can ensure not much goes wrong. The quality of relationship that develops between mentor and trainee deepens as the trainee realizes what public humiliation they've been spared by the wise words of the mentor in advance; but to receive those words takes a good deal of humility from the trainee and to create the conversation takes proactivity from the mentor.

◊ The mentor has to be prepared to relax a bit of control at this stage. That's the difference between stage 1 and stage 2. To relax control at stage 1 is a dereliction of duty; not to do so at all at stage 2 is to risk the goodwill of the trainee. The trainee needs to be able to see their own ideas and skills and insights are being taken seriously and valued.

• Supporting. For many mentors, this is the hardest stage, because it's tempting to lose patience and leave the trainee to their own devices. Among the approaches that can be helpful here are:

◊ To bring together a group of trainees at a similar stage and allow them to compare insights and discoveries and experiences.

◊ To bring in a second mentor, perhaps for a single conversation, who comes from a different perspective—perhaps a "person in the pew."

◊ To encourage the trainee to write down what they believe are the most important things they've learned so far.

◊ To offer a lot of affirmation for the things that are going well.

◊ To look more deeply at the personal motivations and theological significance of the roles of prophet, priest and king, and to look realistically at the projections, costs, and rewards of each.[2]

2. Wells, *God's Companions: Reimagining Christian Ethics.*

- Delegating. This is the point when the senior pastor recognizes things will go as well or better when they themselves aren't there. It's something a senior pastor may find threatening. It separates out those who teach in order to feel their own power, knowledge, and superiority from those who teach in order genuinely to empower people and set them free. It's sometimes said that there are two kinds of teachers, those who seek a forum in which they can exercise control and those who are at heart big kids themselves. Mentoring is best done by the second kind, provided they keep their own needs and playfulness under appropriate restraint. Ministry is an adventure, and the danger for a trainee who thinks they've "cracked it" is to assume because they've learnt how to do it and how to keep people most people happy, they can stop learning. The mentor at this point may find themselves in the opposite role from at stage two: far from reassuring and encouraging, they may need constantly to be drawing into deeper observation, humble repentance, higher aspiration and more careful preparation. Ways to do this include:

  ◊ To expect of oneself what one expects of a trainee. If you ask the trainee to show you their sermon a few days before they deliver it, show them yours on the same timescale and invite comments.

  ◊ To ask the trainee themselves to begin to mentor another trainee, perhaps in a different sphere of ministry. The best way to learn is to teach.

  ◊ To make dates for quarterly reviews and to ask the trainee to do some detailed written preparation that focuses on moments of challenge and how they've been addressed.

The richest territory for reflecting theologically on mentoring and delegating is Jesus' ascension. Ascension Day really is the scariest and most remarkable day in the Christian year. Of course we focus on Christmas—but we preach God with us every Sunday. Of course we focus on Christ risen—but every Sunday is Easter Day. Ascension Day cuts against what we always say. Given that we've seen how God isn't put off by the lowliness of our creaturehood or the depth of our sin, and comes as a baby at Christmas anyway; given that God isn't daunted by the horror of rejection or the prison of death, but comes back to us in the risen Christ on Easter Day, you wonder why Christ can't just hang around with us forever. You can't get a true sense of Ascension Day unless you've had that experience of being tossed in the deep end and set up to fail and have known the panic of feeling alone and way out of your depth. There's a story of a parish secretary who wrote all the pastor's sermons and never got the credit and finally could stand it no longer so one day the pastor was in the pulpit and said, "This is an example of the most complex feature of the human condition as expressed by the great fourth-century theologian . . ." whereupon the pastor turned the page and saw a blank sheet of paper marked only with the words, "You're on your own now." Ascension Day is the day the disciples feel the same panic. They're looking at a blank page where Jesus' words used to be. "You're on your own now." You can feel them looking to left and right and wondering how they can manage the kingdom of God now that it's left to them. Yikes.

In their heads the disciples can look back and realize Christ has been the perfect teacher. He's directed. He's coached. He's supported. And now he's delegated. Fair enough. But in their hearts and guts the disciples are beside themselves. They feel like the teacher in front of the class who never learned the subject, the actor on stage who never learned their lines, the pupil in the exam who never went to any lessons. But deeper than that, even if they could remember what to do, it's not the same. Jesus didn't come to bring a message. Jesus *was* the message: God with us. The disciples weren't inspired by an idea: they were transformed by a person. And now he's gone. They miss him with an ache so deep it's paralyzing, a yearning so profound it's transfixing, a longing so overwhelming it obliterates all rational thought.

We know how the story ends. Ten days after the Ascension the disciples are given something that's not in the education manuals, they discover a stage beyond directing, coaching, supporting and delegating, they find a dimension no other form of learning or formation or training can come anywhere near: they receive the Holy Spirit. Pentecost is well beyond even the best teacher or the most outstanding mentor. Pentecost is the difference between what's possible through the fullest exercise of human reason and what's made possible by God's grace and the gift of faith.

But Pentecost is a good ten days after Ascension. In between lies a period without the glory of Ascension or yet the gift of Pentecost. This mini-season manifests something different from all the other Sundays of the year. Disciples have said goodbye to Jesus but we haven't yet received the Spirit. On fifty-one Sundays of the year Christians celebrate the presence of God, God with us in Jesus through the Holy Spirit. But just this one Sunday after Ascension and before Pentecost Christians feel that ache, that longing, that yearning, that desperate insight into what it's like to be without God. It's scary, humbling, harrowing.

But it demonstrates something tremendously important. It shows us what God feels like most of the time. This one moment of the liturgical year, bereft of Jesus on Ascension Day and not yet clothed with the Spirit at Pentecost, there is a sense we don't know how to get through to God. Every Sunday of the year God wonders how to get through to us. This ache, this longing, this yearning—this is how God feels all the time, when we scorn, betray, wander, reject, discard. And that insight—that window into the heart of God—points us to the true meaning of education, formation, and mentoring. We've talked about eliciting our hidden depths, about information transfer, about training and about formation. We've picked up the key to the wondrous garden of delights and entered a whole new world of discovery and amazement. But the Sunday after Ascension, this vantage-point on God's unrequited longing for us, shows us the ultimate goal of education and mentoring: conversion. Education brings us to the moment when we come face to face with God, and find, not an angry judge, not a merciless tyrant, not an absent-minded uncle, but a pining, aching, longing, yearning heart seeking to be with us now and always, and willing to go to any lengths to make it so. The names of those lengths are Jesus and the Holy Spirit. This is the Sunday we imagine what it would be like to be without either. How we realize our need of both!

And that is the moment of our conversion.

## BIBLIOGRAPHY

Hersey, Paul, and Ken Blanchard. *Management of Organizational Behavior: Utilizing Human Resources.* 3rd ed. Englewood Cliffs, NJ: Prentice Hall 1977.
Wells, Samuel. *God's Companions: Reimagining Christian Ethics.* Oxford: Blackwell, 2006.

# Chapter 5

# Lessons in Change

## PRINCE RIVERS

CIVIL RIGHTS LEADER AND minister Benjamin Hooks said, "If you think you are leading and turn around to see that no one is following, then you are only taking a walk." It might also be true that if we lead and we do not have wise mentors, we are headed for trouble. Research has shown that adolescents with mentors to whom they are not biologically related exhibit more positive attitudes about school, less involvement in high-risk behaviors, and better mental health overall.[1] What if this is also true for pastoral leaders? Could it be the case that our experience of ministry would be more joyous and we would be more resilient and effective over the long haul if we had wise, caring mentors?

Paul's relationship with Timothy comes to mind. Paul had such a deep, personal interest in Timothy that the apostle saw his colleague as a son. Timothy's biological father seems to have had little impact on his life, but Paul encouraged Timothy to follow his good example.

And do you recall what happened in Israel after Solomon died? Solomon's son, Rehoboam, became king and went to Shechem for his coronation. Jeroboam, who fled to Egypt during Solomon's reign, returned to Shechem after hearing the news of Solomon's death. He came to Rehoboam,

1. "Youth-Mentor Relationships," ScienceDaily.

the new king and said, "Your father put a heavy yoke on us, but now lighten the harsh labor and the heavy yoke he put on us, and we will serve you." This was a moment of decision for the new king. How would he handle this transition? Would he maintain the status quo or would he go in a new direction?

Rehoboam first inquired of the elders. The elders were seasoned leaders who advised the king on important matters. They advised Rehoboam to be kind to the people and give them a favorable answer. The elders wanted to preserve the unity of the nation and they realized that to do so Rehoboam needed to proceed with caution. Unfortunately, the new king rejected the counsel of elders to whom he should have looked as his mentors. Sometimes mentors come into our life and we do not receive them, believing they do not know enough to be helpful.

Rehoboam turned aside from the elders and went to young men who had grown up with him and were now serving him. This was the wrong crowd to ask for guidance because unlike genuine mentors these young men were thinking more about their own interests than they were about Rehoboam's. They were royal groupies who probably knew more about the perks of being friends with the king than the responsibility of wisely governing a nation. Rehoboam's young friends told him what sounded good to his own ego. They said, "Now tell [the people], 'My little finger is thicker than my father's waist. My father laid on you a heavy yoke; I will make it heavier. My father scourged you with whips; I will scourge you will scorpions'" (2 Kgs 12:10–11).

Rehoboam's reign was disastrous because he did not choose his mentors wisely. Whenever I read this story, I am even more grateful for the mentors I have had in my life. Like Rehoboam, I have been in the position of succeeding a long-tenured leader. I know firsthand that it is difficult to discern when to maintain the status quo and when to make changes. Without prayer and a few good mentors I would not have known what to do.

United Metropolitan Missionary Baptist Church in Winston-Salem, North Carolina, called me to serve as senior pastor when I was thirty-four years old. My wife and I were excited about the opportunity to begin a new chapter in ministry with our four-month-old son. The former pastor of United Metropolitan had retired one year earlier after serving the congregation for forty-five years. He was (and still is) a legend in North Carolina Baptist life. The congregation was healthy, but transition always comes with unforeseen challenges. I gave an interview to a journalist not long after arriving in Winston-Salem, and the first thing the reporter said to me was, "You've some big shoes to fill." No pressure, right?

One of the first members to visit my office gave me a tiny slip of paper on which was a typed quotation.

> There is nothing more difficult to manage, more dubious to accomplish nor more doubtful of success than to initiate a new order of things. The reformer has enemies in all those who profit from the old order and only lukewarm defenders in all those who would profit from the new order.

The quote is attributed to Machiavelli and it remains taped to the edge of my desk where it has been for ten years. As I write this chapter, the tape is peeling and the paper's edges have turned yellow. These words have served as a reminder to me about the hazards of leading change.

Congregational leadership is challenging for a number of reasons. Pastors have to lead without the typical forms of leverage that leaders have in secular organizations. Funding is often an unpredictable resource. The skills required to lead a congregation are not always the skills we mastered in seminary. Take your pick.

When I look back on ministry at United Metropolitan and six years as senior pastor in two other congregations before coming to Winston-Salem, I can say that I have enjoyed success and experienced failure. The failures I attribute mostly to my own impatience or lack of discernment. The successes have everything to do with the grace of God and the ministry of the wonderful people who have come in and out of my life as friends and mentors, both in person and through the written word. Mentors coached me in how to wisely practice the art of leadership, especially in the context of congregational change. When I listened to their sage counsel I enjoyed the benefits of looking much smarter than I was at the time. In the next several paragraphs I will share lessons I have learned from my mentors. I hope that those who have been called to congregational leadership might find strength for the journey.

## STAYING GROUNDED

One of the earliest mentors in my ministry taught me about staying spiritually grounded. The Christian life cannot be lived well without a vibrant spiritual connection. Jesus told the disciples, "No branch can bear fruit by itself; it must remain in the vine. Neither can you bear fruit unless you remain in me" (John 15:4).

Lewis Anthony, a pastor in the AME Zion Church, impressed me with his life of prayer before I began seminary. We met for the first time in a restaurant where I worked. He took an interest in my preparation for ministry. Pastor Anthony gave me books to read and taught me to live a life of prayer (even though I did not know he was doing so at the time). Anthony introduced me to the works of Henri Nouwen, who wrote wisely on this: "Through the discipline of contemplative prayer we can keep ourselves from being pulled from one urgent issue to another and from becoming strangers to our own and God's heart."[2]

Anthony's favorite reminder to me was, "Stay on your knees and in the Book." At first, I thought this was the quaint advice of a pastor who did not understand the demands on contemporary ministers. Today's pastors are called to be administrators, communicators, and community change agents. We have to manage budgets, attract newer and younger members, and be relevant to our times. However, it did not take me long to realize that Anthony knew exactly what was required of modern ministers, which was precisely why he offered that simple yet profound reminder: "Stay on your knees and in the Book."

Mentors I have known personally, like Lewis Anthony, taught me how to pray. Mentors I have known through the written page have reinforced this invaluable lesson. The Reverend Paul Smith was my pastor during my childhood. He loved to read the writings of Howard Thurman and knew Thurman personally. Consequently, Thurman's insights often appeared in his sermons. Years later, as a college student and then as a seminarian, Thurman became a companion and mentor in my devotional life. While I do travel with many other spiritual friends as I pray, I enjoy Thurman because he helps me to slow down and savor each word from God and to God. He encourages me to be patient and notice God at work everywhere.

I visited Paul in New York after accepting my call to ministry and before I started divinity school. He was pastoring in Brooklyn at the time. At the end of our conversation I asked him what advice he had for a young minister. Paul told me, "Be true to yourself." I must admit that I had really expected to hear something else from someone who had been in ministry for decades. Maybe I was expecting something more spiritual like, "Save for retirement!"

2. Nouwen, *In the Name of Jesus*, 29.

Over the years, I have learned to value these words. Paul's counsel has saved me from many "dangers, toils, and snares." The temptation to be someone we are not is present in ministry just like it is in every other vocation. Paul's wisdom has helped me to remain spiritually grounded as I have changed pastorates and moved to different cities. This has been especially true of my transition to a congregation where a member in his late forties told me that my pastoral predecessor was the only pastor he had ever known. In that moment it became important for me to heed Paul's admonition to be true to myself. If I had set out to emulate someone else in order to win the approval of others, I would have been rendered impotent by a lack of authenticity. Fortunately, the congregation and I learned to accept each other as we were and we have both grown and changed along the way.

## MAKING CHANGE

When I first started pastoring I thought that congregational change was the exception. For some reason I believed that once you made a few tweaks the church eventually arrived at a place where change was no longer necessary or at least not the norm. Now I know that change is the rule. Everything that is alive is changing. God is a God of change—from creation to new creation, and from Egypt to Exodus. Mentors have taught me how to thrive in a culture of change. My late uncle, Reverend G. Wesley Raney III, once gave me a book on church administration. I do not remember the name of the book, but I do remember what he wrote on the inside cover. "Rome wasn't built in a day!" He knew that I would be constantly engaged in the work of change, but he did not want me to become frustrated with the pace of change as it occurs in most congregations. He was so right.

Most of the time, I have been good about listening to the advice of people I respect. My uncle had my highest respect so I did not plan to make changes quickly at the second congregation I served, which was in Newport News, Virginia. But much to my surprise, in my relatively short tenure change happened all over the place. In the first six months, we changed the choirs' Sunday schedule. In the first year, a key lay leader changed, as did the decor of the church's education wing. We changed the order of service and introduced a vision statement. God allowed these wonderful changes to happen in a span of less than three years. Maybe Rome was not built in a day, but we sure did a lot in three years.

However, when I reflect on my third year of ministry in Winston-Salem, not much had changed at all from the time I arrived. We were using the same order of service. The church was adding new members, but we were also having funerals at an alarming rate so attendance was not changing much. I found a wise mentor in the writings of John Kotter, a business school professor.

Kotter's book *Leading Change* suggests that the first task of the leader is not to cast vision but to create a sense of urgency. People must affirm that idea that change is needed. Too often leaders attempt to make change, but no one has any sense of urgency that the change is necessary. This insight opened up a whole new way for me to understand the dynamics of congregational change. When a pastor comes to a congregation that is aware of the need for change, he or she has tacit permission to make *some* change fairly quickly. This is what happened to me in Newport News. When a pastor comes to a congregation that needs change (which all congregations do) but is not aware of its need for change, he or she does not have permission, implicit or explicit, to make change. In the first scenario, a church will learn to trust the pastor based on how well the changes work. In the second scenario, a pastor must first earn trust before he or she can make substantial changes. One must know how to exegete the congregational context to know the difference.

I knew when I came to United Metropolitan, I was in a wonderful, vibrant congregation that did not collectively perceive a need for change. They wanted improvement, but there is a difference between improvement and change. Improvement usually involves doing more of what we are already doing. Change involves rethinking and reworking what we are doing and making room for something new.

There have been times when I knew I needed to do something new, but I also needed to respect and value what was already in place. One of the principles of change I picked up from a short but insightful book by E. Stanley Ott is "bless and add."[3] New pastors often try to make change by eliminating one thing to make way for the new. We have to remember that no matter how much we think the old program (structure, paradigm, etc.) needs to go, it is probably important to someone. We will not know how important it is until we try to bury it. So Ott advocates the practice of "bless and add."

3. Ott, *Twelve Dynamic Shifts*, 22.

With Ott as my mentor, one of the first changes we made at United Metropolitan was to start a new worship service. I really wanted to make changes to the existing service, but did not have enough consensus to do so without tearing the congregation apart. So we started a second service in the chapel at an earlier time than our existing worship service. A few years later, the early service outgrew the chapel and had to be moved to the main sanctuary. We never had to critique the existing service. We simply blessed it as it was and added a new service. Ten years later, our two services have changed. They are identical and both are well attended enough to be held in the sanctuary. Anyone leading change in a congregation should consider the practice of blessing and adding.

## A LESSON IN DYING

All change in a congregation does not happen at the level of systems or programs. Some change affects individual members of the church in deeply personal ways. One such change that is inevitable is death. We need mentors to show us how to lead people through despair into hope. I learned a pivotal lesson in ministry when my father died. I moved my father, who was suffering from Parkinson's disease, to Winston-Salem. The congregation welcomed my dad with open arms. The church van brought him to worship every Sunday and he enjoyed all of the special attention he received for being the preacher's dad. After church one Sunday, I listened to a voicemail from the woman who cared for my dad. She wanted me to know that he did not look well. We took my dad to the hospital where he was admitted for "failure to thrive." He was conscious the first few days, but then he became less coherent as vital organs shut down.

Having been with families in similar situations so many times, I knew that he was dying. I found privacy on a park bench outside of the hospital and called Paul Smith, my childhood pastor and my dad's dear friend. As soon as he picked up the phone, I began sobbing uncontrollably. Finally, I didn't have to be "strong." I could be a grieving son, which is what I needed to be. Paul drove to Winston-Salem the next day. Not only did he minister to me; he mentored me in the art of caring for the dying and their families. He knew that my sisters and I needed him to be with us, but he also knew we needed our own space to grieve in our own way. Paul's ministry to me was a wonderful example of how to serve Christians and their families at the end of life. I had been in the place of doing so before, but never had

I been mentored by such a wise and gentle soul. Paul showed me how to be a good pastor in the valley of the shadow of death. I am a better pastor because he took the time to show up. I am forever grateful.

## WISDOM BELONGS TO THE CHURCH

One day in seminary, my friends went to hear one of our favorite professors preach in a chapel service. We enjoyed the message so much that we approached him afterwards to tell him how much his words meant to us. I jokingly told him that I was going to use his material one day. He smiled confidently and said, "Please do. It belongs to the church!"

I loved hearing that. Our professor was by no means encouraging us to plagiarize his or anyone else's sermons. He was merely acknowledging that we are all a part of something bigger than ourselves. The wisdom is not something we cling to and hoard as if it is a finite resource. The wisdom we have is meant to be shared. It is not ours alone. It belongs to the church. This is what I think about when I consider the importance of receiving and being a mentor. Whatever wisdom we have belongs to the church. I am grateful for all I have received and humbled whenever I can share with others.

## BIBLIOGRAPHY

"Youth-Mentor Relationships Particularly Helpful for those Experiencing Hardship." ScienceDaily. www.sciencedaily.com/releases/2011/05/110512171527.htm.
Kotter, John P. *Leading Change*. Boston: Harvard Business School Press, 1996.
Nouwen, Henri. *In the Name of Jesus: Reflections on Christian Leadership*. New York: Crossroad, 1989.
Ott, Stanley. *Twelve Dynamic Shifts for Transforming Your Church*. Grand Rapids: Eerdmans, 2002.

# Chapter 6

# The Gifts of Mentors in Ministry

## WILL WILLIMON

MY FIRST WEEK AS a college freshman they forced us to read Homer's *Odyssey*. When a fellow student had the temerity to ask why read so ancient a book, the professor shot back, "You're nineteen. You should have noted that the *Odyssey*'s climax occurs when Odysseus, having abandoned his wife and son to wander over the Aegean with his buddies, finally returns home. His son, Telemachus, has been wisely entrusted to the care of Mentor, a disguise for Athena, goddess of wisdom. Get it? You can't grow up by yourself. Find a wise mentor to guide you out of the morass of your adolescence."

Growing up is tough; an even greater challenge is to be a faithful disciple of Jesus Christ. Ministry in the name of Jesus is too demanding for solo performance.[1] Jesus therefore sent out the seventy-two in mis-

---

1. That nearly all of the research and most of the thoughtful books on mentoring (with the exception of this volume!) are from business and academia is judgment upon the too-limited practice of pastoral leadership done by many clergy. For the best of mentoring research, see Ragins and Kram, *Handbook of Mentoring at Work: Theory, Research, and Practice*; Zey, *The Mentor Connection: Strategic Alliances in Corporate Life*; and Felten, *Transformative Conversations: Guide to Mentoring Communities among Colleagues in Higher Education*. The best handbook on educational mentoring seems to be Zachary, *The Mentor's Guide: Facilitating Effective Learning Relationship*.

sion, "two by two" (Luke 10:1–16). Paul and Barnabas worked together, an older, more experienced disciple tutoring the younger. Many of Paul's letters could be construed as forms of mentoring, not only his letters to Timothy. Then there's Ambrose and Augustine, Luther and Melanchthon, Wesley and Whitfield, Martin Luther King and Benjamin Mays, or for that matter, Will Willimon and Bessie Parker. Something inherent in ministry makes it necessary to undertake Christian leadership two by two.[2] We may be among the first generation of pastors in five centuries who not only must care for a congregation but also transform the church. It is foolhardy for anyone to attempt to be a mission leader in the name of Christ without the supervision, accountability, support, advice, humor, and receptivity that characterize good mentoring.[3]

I think of mentoring as a subspecies of the genus, *conversation*, specifically, guided conversation between a more experienced guide and a less experienced protégé who are friends.[4] As in any good conversation virtues like honesty, focus, self-revelation, risk, and engagement are important. As in any good *friendship*, commitment to mutual growth of the friend feeds friendship along with the daring willingness to be changed by the friend. As with friendship or conversation, mentoring is most effective when it is sustained over time. I have been a seminary teacher to many but a mentor only to a few who invited me to be a continuing contributor to their developing vocation, some of these clergy are editors of and contributors to this volume.

Over four decades into ministry, I've both learned some things and have received some gifts as a mentor:

*Mentoring is a fierce, focused, continuing conversation in which a mentor, attempting to be helpful to a protégé, is helped.*

Just about everything Jesus accomplished was through the typically Jewish medium of nonviolent but powerful words. Upon being elected as Bishop of the church, I spent some time with a mentor who teaches in the Fuqua School of Business at Duke. "What is the church asking you to do in this new job?" he asked. After my rambling account of my new duties he shoved a book at me. "Leadership is the art of talking people into things. You lead only as far as words can take you. Scott can teach you how."

---

2. Floding, "Fostering a Mentoring Environment," 272–81.

3. Blodgett, *Pastor You Hope to Be*, 23.

4. Daloz, et al., *Common Fire*, 45.

Susan Scott's *Fierce Conversations*[5] increased my awareness that all relationships, all leadership, all transformation is through words. Mindfulness about asking more questions than offering answers, intense listening, and curiosity about what is *not* being said in the conversation are among the skills that Scott teaches. She urges more candor about what we are unable to hear in a conversation rather than what we are able to say. Scott shows that a major reason why we don't hear the words of others is that we fear the painful, costly change that courageous listening often provokes.

Philosopher Theodore Zeldin[6] believes that the mutual, often costly, conversational give-and-take that occurs between two persons is essential to all human creativity. Indeed, Zeldin prefers not to speak of "creativity" but prefers instead "procreativity"—what two people can do together that they cannot accomplish as lone individuals. Opposing both the myth of the heroic individual inventor and the myth of heroic, collective, mass action, Zeldin says that conversation between two individuals who dare to transcend their individuality is the primary generator of human creativity and ingenuity. In conversation, we have the greatest likelihood of understanding one another, influencing one another, and being mutually changed in the process. Isolation, a byproduct of romantic individualism, stifles creativity and truthfulness. New insights and solutions are the fruit of intense, focused, risky conversation, says Zeldin, not of lonely, introspective brooding. Free from the tyranny of the limitations of marriage, parents, and family, fierce conversations with a friend enable us to think better than we could on our own. Citing historical examples of the procreativity of two friends, Zeldin shows that most of the really creative acts of genius in human history are ignited and fueled two-by-two, as gracious byproducts of the practice of friendship.

Jolene Cassellius Erlacher documents that mentoring is especially important for the professional development of millennials in ministry.[7] My generation's mantra was, famously, "Don't trust anyone over thirty." Something within the lives of the present under-forty crowd craves friendship with older, experienced practitioners of the craft of ministry. Identification of one's strengths and weaknesses, articulation of one's goals, discovery of talent, surprise at the work of the Holy Spirit within one's human work,

---

5. Scott, *Fierce Conversations*.

6. Zeldin, *The Hidden Pleasures of Life*.

7. Erlacher, *Millennials in Ministry*.

embrace of one's God-given vocation are among the gifts that mentors can give developing clergy.

Pastoral ministry is intensely public, an exercise of power, therefore a mentor's acquisition of self-knowledge is essential. Conversation tends to be most candid when it is conducted in a safe environment where the protégé feels free to express thoughts that may otherwise need to be suppressed. It's helpful to keep mutually clear about the rules of engagement, and keep asking, "Did we talk about what you wanted to process today?" Otherwise, the mentoring conversation is little more than a social relationship and a polite chit chat.

While it's true that mentoring requires time and energy, looking back over my own experience as a mentor, I'm impressed by the many gifts that I received as a mentor. In mentoring conversations the mentor is forced to articulate the principles and understandings under which the mentor has worked. In teaching, we are taught. Self-examination and self-evaluation occur. This can be humbling. How well I remember the protégé who asked, while we were talking about whether or not she should leave the pastoral ministry, "You want to encourage me to stay, but *you* left for college chaplaincy. I don't think you are being straight with me about all that you gained by leaving?" Thus have *my protégés made me a more honest person than I would have been if I had been left to my own devices.*

One of my students began a conversation by flattering me with, "You are the only faculty member who has shown interest in me. Could I get your advice on a subject that is really bothering me?" I was eager to help.

He then told me that he and his wife had grown up in relatively affluent families. They liked nice things and had always had everything they needed and most of what they had wanted. He said that they had prayed about the challenge of his becoming a Methodist pastor and being forced to live on a meager salary the rest of their lives. He wondered if they were up to the challenge of low income.

I praised the student for his honesty and told him how important it was to ponder the financial constraints of ministry.

He continued, "I've noted, on the Methodist website, that your last year as bishop you made over a hundred thousand dollars. How did you and your wife think about the moral dangers of that sort of salary?"

That conversation demonstrated the challenge of being someone's mentor!

*Mentoring is essential for the professional growth and deepening faith of the mentor.*

Secular literature tends to define mentoring as a personal relationship in which a person who is more experienced and older acts as guide, role model, teacher, and sponsor/advocate for a protégé who is less experienced and younger. But I can testify to the joy that comes from allowing a younger person to be guide, teacher, and sometimes advocate for the mentor.

One of the chief challenges of being a bishop, when compared with my previous life as a university chaplain, was being forced constantly to be with people over sixty. (The median age of United Methodists is sixty.) I had to admit how much I receive from being a mentor to the young. Not only was I given a privileged peek at the church of the future but also the great compliment of a new church leader thinking that my ministry was worth his or her emulation.

Psychologists asked protégés to list characteristics of an effective mentor. They most frequently mentioned supportive, intelligent, knowledgeable, ethical, caring, humorous, encouraging and honest, nonsexist, flexible, loyal.[8] Allow me to turn the tables and ask, as a mentor, "What are the virtues of effective mentees?" Chief on my list of characteristics of the successful protégé is willingness to contribute to the growth of an older, more experienced friend. I've asked, at the beginning of a mentoring relationship, "Are you sure that you want me to know a great deal about you and are you willing to know more about me? Right now, I appear to be someone whom you like and admire. Are you willing to see my flaws and shortcomings?"

As in any form of teaching, mentoring requires the astute, careful, responsible exercise of power. One reason why some avoid being cast as mentors is that they do not wish to assume the burden of power over another person's life. (I once had a student write me, "Well, I did just what you advised me to do. Afterwards, the Board met, took a vote, and now I'm looking for a job. Got any other bright ideas?").

Inept mentoring can be dangerous when power is abused by the mentor. Some of the ethically questionable lapses in my own mentoring are when I have: attempted to bolster my own ego by assuming the role of an expert in areas over which I lacked true expertise; gossiped or derided my colleagues in order to ingratiate myself with my protégé; failed to question and listen in such a way that gave me a sufficiently thick and nuanced

8. Wilson, "Core Virtues," 2, 121.

understanding of the situation under discussion; lacked a clear sense of what my protégé was asking from me in the discussion; and failed to appreciate the differences between my own goals and gifts and those of my protégé.

When Aristotle reflected upon the necessary qualities of the teacher, he stressed not only self-knowledge but also that a teacher must be willing to be taught. Mentoring is a process of *mutual* growth, a give-and-take conversation in which one of the most important qualities of the mentor is an *eagerness to grow, to learn, and to be assessed by a younger protégé.*[9] Mentoring is more a relationship than a role with preconceived duties, a mutually enriching educational journey. Any profession advances and adapts through the constant induction of new members into the profession who, even as they are being formed into the practices of the profession, critique and transform the profession.

"Some friends play at friendship but a true friend sticks closer than one's nearest kin" (Prov 18:24 NRSV). The main thing we offer a protégé is ourselves; everything else they need to know about ministry can be obtained from a book. (Though to be sure reading a good book is much like being under the guidance of a mentor.) A major gift of higher education (and one that is sadly lacking in many of the practices of the modern university[10]) is to allow students to look over the shoulders of faculty elders. A major threat of being faculty is to be exposed to the penetrating stare of the young!

As I was telling a protégé about some of the important work I was doing on a denominational board, he disarmingly asked, "Did you find that your tolerance for boring meetings increased as you got older?" Ouch!

I'm the right age to note that the opportunity to be a mentor may be a positive contributor to aging gracefully. George Valliant, in his analysis of the findings of the Grant Study of Harvard graduates from the Class of 1939, identifies common characteristics of men in their eighties who have, according to Valliant's criteria, aged successfully. Valliant cites the willingness "to foster and guide the next generations," particularly the young who are not members of one's own family, as a major contributor to successful aging in men.[11] Earlier, Erik Erikson praised the willingness to contribute

9. Orland-Barak and Hasin, "Exemplary Mentors' Perspectives," 429.

10. Naylor and Willimon, *Abandoned Generation*. See my polemic against the distancing of faculty from students.

11. Valliant, *Triumphs of Experience*, 154–55.

to the self-development of the young as "generativity" (as opposed to "stagnation") in which a mature adult grew and developed by the "assumption of sustained responsibility for the growth and well-being" of the young who are not our children.[12]

*Mentoring is peculiarly essential for the faithful formation of effective pastors.*

Lily Orland-Barak and Ronit Hasin studied the responses of star mentors in education in Israel and found that excellent educational mentors are peculiarly adept at "organizational skills, interpersonal relationships, integration of theory and practice, knowledge and expertise, challenge, modelling and reflexivity."[13] We should not be surprised that the pastoral ministry, in which pastors are mainly teachers, can affirm this list as well. But what are the peculiarly Christian virtues that make for good mentors of those called to service by the church?

Recently I read through a dozen autobiographies of renowned pastors and noted in every case the importance of a developing pastor having a mentor. Eugene Peterson's citation of and gratitude for his mentors in his *Pastor*[14] is typical. Earlier, in his *Contemplative Pastor*,[15] Peterson advised that the most important step in receiving apt spiritual direction was selection of a wise mentor. Something about service in the name of Jesus requires mentoring. Perhaps sustained, focused, transformative friendship is required because our vocation is always external—our ministry is God's idea before it is ours. To paraphrase Kierkegaard, the call to Christian ministry does not arise from any human heart; we are in ministry through external imposition of the twofold vocation from God and the church.

As I see it, we are the first generation of pastors in a century to be forced—by the demands of a living God, the desperate need of the church, and our changed cultural context—not only to care for the congregation but also to lead the church. Unfortunately, *few of us had training in the best practices and proven means of leadership and management.* Seminarians complain about the lack of leadership courses. Yet few seminary faculty have experience or insight into this demanding area of pastoral work.[16] To those newly minted pastors who lament their lack of preparation effectively

---

12. Erikson, *Childhood and Society,* 272.

13. Orland-Barak and Hasin, "Exemplary Mentors' Perspectives," 427–37.

14. Peterson, *The Pastor.*

15. Peterson, *Contemplative Pastor.*

16. Wimberly, *Business of Church.*

to lead, my standard prescription is, "Get you a mentor." For women in ministry, dealing daily with the pressures of sexism, mentoring is especially important, though in some denominations finding good role models among the comparatively few women clergy can be difficult.[17]

Gregory the Great argued that he was unsuited for the pastoral vocation because he loved the solitary monastic life and pastors are in the most public (and political) of roles. Anything a pastor accomplishes is through relationships and influence (alas, God has given us pastors neither an army nor even a cattle prod to force our people to follow us). The interpersonal demands of ministry require that we gain self-knowledge, particularly knowledge of how we interact with fellow Christians. That sort of knowledge can only come through sustained, critical, sometimes fierce conversation with a friend who is trusted and who has taken the time to get to know us down deep.

One of the reasons why, in my seminary courses, I try to organize my students into learning teams, giving them assignments that must be completed as a team, is that I'm convinced that an essential requirement for future clergy is *the ability to give and to receive help.* The director of our clergy psychological support services told me that she has never had a clergyperson lapse into clergy misconduct who was not also a lonely person. A clergyperson without friends is not only on ethically dangerous ground (Aristotle defines an immoral person as a person without friends, a detached individual who lacks anyone to correct him) but also a pastor who lacks the resources necessary to grow as a pastor.

It's important for the pastoral mentor and protégé to acknowledge that *we work under the aegis of Scripture.* We are accountable to standards and goals that transcend (and sometimes call into question) our personal career trajectories. Thus the mentor may ask questions like, "Can you think of any Scripture that speaks to your present situation?" One of the proudest moments in my own mentoring was when I told a young pastor, after a long conversation about whether or not he ought to call it quits in ministry, to go home a spend a week reading through Jeremiah before he did anything rash. At the end of the week he called and said that his reading had convinced him that, "I'm nobody special. Jeremiah said worse things to God than I would ever say and still he stayed with God. I'm here for the duration."

---

17. Rayburn and Reuder, *Handbook for Women Mentors.*

In our dealings with Scripture, and in Scripture's dealings with us, the text stokes, funds, and fuels our imagination. One of the reasons why a protégé seeks the guidance of a mentor is to receive a wider array of options than those that appear to be available through the protégé's comparatively limited experience. Scripture keeps expanding our horizon and reframing our situation.

A Jewish Duke student told me of his frustration in seeking guidance from our campus rabbi. "I tell him about my problem, then he spends the rest of the time telling me stories from the rabbis. When I complain to him about not getting any answers he says, 'Look kid, my job is to tell you true stories; your job is to figure out how to live like a Jew. I'm forty years older than you. It's your world now, not mine, so what do I know about what you ought to do? We're Jews for God's sake! My job is to be sure you know the right stories; your job is to live them.'"

Because we are servants of God and not God, pastors will find that a great resource in a mentoring relationship is *humor.* I agree with Reinhold Niebuhr that sin is taking ourselves too seriously. Pastors have lots of opportunities seriously to sin. I vividly recall pouring out my heart to one of my own mentors, sadly cataloging my repeated failures to bring my rural Georgia congregation into the promised land, only to have my mentor reply, "Congratulations. You've learned that you are not the Messiah."

"I meant that I haven't found the right way to get across what we need to do and . . ." I continued.

"You've found out that, in spite of all your gifts, you are not their Savior. I guess Jesus will just have to save them since you can't." Thank God for the gift of being able to sit lightly on our ministry.

In a cruciform faith, *sometimes it's difficult to tell the difference between success and failure.* In the practice of ministry, mentors need not be surprised that they praise a protégé for leadership that he or she believed to be a flop or to raise difficult questions when the protégé expects to be praised. Following a God who was driven out of the world on a cross (Luther) much of our mentoring will be comforting a protégé during times of dismal failure.

Most of the secular literature on mentoring stresses the need for confidentiality. For those in pastoral ministry, confidentiality after sensitive conversations is just another day at the office. However, this emphasis on keeping confidence in mentoring reminds us Christians that a gift we have is the dynamic of *confession/forgiveness* inherent in our faith. No Christian mentor or protégé ought to be surprised at the presence of mixed motives and unspoken, self-serving intentions in our conversations or in our ministries. In short, we ought to expect the presence of *sin* in the mentoring relationship, attempt to name the sin and confess it when it occurs, then to be thankful that a redemptive God loves to bring something good out of our screw ups.

Which leads me to perhaps the most important and (in my own mentoring) underutilized gifts in specifically Christian mentoring: *prayer*. In prayer the faithful mentor and protégé frame our conversation within the parameters of our vocation. We pray for the willingness to let God be God in God's own good time, asking God to fix what we can't figure out, then to take our faltering ministries and weave them into God's good purposes. In prayer God graciously gives us bright ideas that we could not think up on our own. As Christians, we never work alone. Our actions, for good or ill, are not the whole story. The lives we live are not our own. We have been commandeered. Prayer, which I define as conversation with God, enables the conversation that is the mentoring relationship to open up to the wider purposes of God, to have our little lives swept up into the great pageant that is, "Thy Kingdom come, Thy will be done on earth as in heaven."

## BIBLIOGRAPHY

Blodgett, Barbara. *Becoming the Pastor You Hope to Be: Four Practices for Improving Ministry.* Herndon, VA: Alban Institute, 2011.

Daloz, Laurent A. Parks, et al. *Common Fire: Leading Lives of Commitment in Complex World.* Boston: Beacon, 1996.

Erikson, Erik H. *Childhood and Society.* 2nd ed. New York: Norton, 1963.

Erlacher, Jolene Cassellius. *Millennials in Ministry.* Valley Forge, PA: Judson, 2014.

Felten, Peter, et al. *Transformative Conversations: Guide to Mentoring Communities among Colleagues in Higher Education.* San Francisco: Jossey-Bass, 2013.

Floding, Matthew. "Fostering a Mentoring Environment." *Reflective Practice: Formation Supervision in Ministry* 32 (2012) 272–81. http://journals.sfu.ca/rpfs/index.php/rpfs/article/view/77.

Naylor, Thomas H., and William H. Willimon. *Abandoned Generation: Rethinking Higher Education.* Grand Rapids: Eerdmans, 1995.

Orland-Barak, Lily, and Ronit Hasin. "Exemplary Mentors' Perspectives towards Mentoring across Mentoring Contexts: Lessons from Collective Case Studies." *Teaching and Teacher Education* 26 (2010) 427–37.

Peterson, Eugene H. *Contemplative Pastor: Returning to Art of Spiritual Direction.* Grand Rapids: Eerdmans. 1993.

———. *The Pastor: A Memoir.* New York: HarperOne, 2011.

Ragins, Belle Rose, and Kathy E. Kram. *The Handbook of Mentoring at Work: Theory, Research, and Practice.* Los Angeles: Sage, 2007.

Rayburn, Carole A., et al. *A Handbook for Women Mentors: Transcending Barriers of Stereotype, Race, and Ethnicity.* New York: Praeger. 2010.

Scott, Susan. *Fierce Conversations: Achieving Success at Work and Life, One Conversation at Time.* New York: Penguin, 2002.

Valliant, George E. *Triumphs of Experience: Men of Harvard Grant Study.* Cambridge, MA: Belknap Press of Harvard University Press. 2012.

Wilson, Peter F. "Core Virtues for the Practice of Mentoring." *Journal of Psychology and Theology* 29 (2001) 121–30.

Wimberly, John. *The Business of the Church: The Uncomfortable Truth That Faithful Ministry Requires Effective Management.* Herndon, VA: Alban Institute, 2010.

Zachary, Lois J. *The Mentor's Guide: Facilitating Effective Learning Relationships.* 2nd ed. San Francisco: Jossey-Bass, 2011.

Zeldin, Theodore, *The Hidden Pleasures of Life: A New Way of Remembering the Past and Imagining the Future.* London: MacLehose, 2015.

Zey, Michael G. *The Mentor Connection: Strategic Alliances in Corporate Life.* London: Transaction, 1991.

# Introduction to Chapter 7

# Leighton Ford
## Artist of the Soul and Friend on the Journey

### KEN SHIGEMATSU

LEIGHTON FORD WAS A star in the Christian world. From the 1950s to the 1980s, he was preaching in large football stadiums around the world. He was named by the Religious Heritage of America as Clergyman of the Year, and *Time* magazine identified him as the person most qualified to succeed his famous brother-in-law, Billy Graham.

Leighton also had a son named Sandy. An accomplished track and field runner in his teenage years, Sandy was diagnosed with a rare heart disease that caused an irregular heartbeat. An operation seemed to fix the problem, and Sandy began studying at the University of North Carolina at Chapel Hill. He became a student leader and, like his father, aspired to become a minister of the gospel. The disease returned, however, and shortly after he turned 21 Sandy died on an operating table.

In the midst of this deep loss, Leighton sensed God calling him to begin a new ministry away from the limelight, preaching not to stadiums but focusing instead on a small group of young men and women through one-on-one spiritual mentoring.

To the outside observer, Leighton's new ministry was humbler and much lower-key than when he was a rock-star stadium evangelist with the

Billy Graham team. But as Leighton walks with a smaller number of people as "an artist of the soul and a friend on the journey," the ripple effect of his life and influence extends around the world and into eternity as his young mentees are empowered "to lead more like Jesus and more to Jesus."

My first significant encounter with Leighton was when I was a seminary student in Boston. He asked if I would drive him west across Massachusetts, to the home of a board member of his ministry. I picked up Leighton at about 10 p.m. from Logan International Airport. As I merged onto the interstate, I turned to him and said, "You can recline your chair and sleep if you want." Leighton crossed his long legs, reclined the chair part-way and said, "I don't think I'll sleep . . . tell me your life story." That invitation sparked a friendship. For more than two decades, Leighton has been available as an attentive friend on my journey.

When I arrived at Tenth Church in Vancouver, British Columbia, as a young senior pastor in the summer of 1996, I was intimidated by the challenge of pastoring a historic church that had seen its glory years in the 1950s. Since then, church attendance had dwindled from more than 1,000 to a hundred-and-something people who were largely elderly, and primarily of European ancestry. The church had cycled through twenty pastors (including associates) in twenty years. All of them, it seemed to me, were far more experienced and gifted than I was, yet none of them had been able to halt what seemed like the slow and inevitable death of the church.

Leighton came to visit a couple of weeks after my arrival. We were sitting in my car not far from the church. I felt a desperate need for encouragement, but I was too ashamed to ask. Instead, I asked for some counsel. Leighton paused and said, "Remember that God is an artist. He will not lead you to copy anyone else. Seek God for his unique vision for this place."

Not only in my pastoral ministry, but whenever I have been at a crossroads or at a significant milestone, Leighton has been present and mediated Christ's love and wisdom to me.

When my fiancé and I had broken up and I was in despair, his presence and genuine care became the most tangible expression of God's face to me.

When I was about to get married (to a different woman) he joyfully officiated our wedding.

When I was feeling burned out, Leighton invited me on a pilgrimage to the holy places of Ireland, a journey that was not only life-giving but sowed the seeds for my first book—a book he encouraged me to write, trusting my voice even when I didn't.

Leighton's mentoring has been, and remains, whole-life and life-long.

To echo the words of the Apostle Paul, I have had many teachers, but Leighton Ford became my father in Christ.

# Chapter 7

# Mentoring
## The Ministry of a Lifetime

### LEIGHTON FORD

MY MENTORING STORY BEGAN long before I knew I was being mentored, or even knew the word.

The best way for me to tell this story is through some key figures and times in my life.

## ABANDONMENT AND INVITATION

I was fourteen years old, and the year had been both very hard and very encouraging.

My adopted mother, Olive, who was both very devout and very troubled, had left home early in the year and gone to live in Winnipeg under an assumed name. I later realized she was suffering from severe paranoia, and very afraid that my father, who was her partner in their jewelry store, was going to harm her in some way.

Mom came back in late spring, but that sense of being left alone stayed.

That summer a new Bible conference opened nearby and I went with some friends. I liked the other young people there, was infatuated with a pretty hostess, and was moved by the speaker of the week, Oswald Smith. He told us how, since he was nervous and easily distracted, he prayed by walking up and down, praying out loud, and turning verses from the Psalms into words of prayer.

The next morning I took my Bible into the nearby woods, and prayed in the way he described. I don't remember exactly the Scripture verses that spoke to me. I do remember sensing God's presence and care for this lonely fourteen year old.

That September, 1946, a man came to Chatham to promote the Canadian Youth Fellowship, a forerunner of Youth for Christ. Evon Hedley looked more like a business man than a preacher. He inspired a small group of us, meeting in a storefront church, that we should organize youth rallies to reach our friends for Christ.

That night my friend Danny nominated me as president and Evon confirmed the appointment. He had assumed I was seventeen, because I was tall. When he found out I was only fourteen he must have nearly had a heart attack!

But Evon stuck with us, and with me. He sent speakers our way. Gave me ideas. Set up my first speaking opportunities for me. Took me to national conferences and introduced me to the leaders. He scolded me once when I didn't show up for an appointment. Later after I began my ministry of evangelism he introduced me to people who would become lifelong teammates.

I didn't know that Evon was "mentoring" me. But he was a way-opener for this young lad.

As I write Evon is ninety-seven, living in southern California, and still mentoring younger men!

## DISAPPOINTMENT AND PRAYER

It's a cold, icy southern Ontario night. The roads are frozen over. But in spite of the weather the largest crowd ever to attend one of our local Youth for Christ rallies has packed our vocational school auditorium.

They have come from miles around to hear a young evangelist from the southern United States, Billy Graham, who is already well known for his forceful, dynamic messages.

We have put up posters all over the county, sent word around to the churches, put ads in the paper. We have prayed long and hard and invited all our friends who as far as we know are not true "Christians." We are sure that for many of them this night will be their hour of decision.

Billy's message does not disappoint. With a long pointing finger, dramatic gestures, a piercing voice and long, stretched-out southern syllables he warns, "Prepaa .. hhh to meet Thy God."

Then he gives his invitation. The piano plays. We sing. He waits.

No one comes. He waits. Commands again, "You come." No one does. There is a painful silence. We shift in our seats. Pray more. Still no one comes. Finally one twelve-year old timidly walks to the front to rededicate her life to the Lord.

Billy prays for her. It's over. People leave.

I am devastated. I needn't have been, for that young girl later served the Lord in ministry. But we had expected everyone to respond. Cold, reserved Canadians that we were, public displays of faith were difficult. I knew that. But still it wasn't what I had hoped for.

As the crowd left I went to the wings of the stage, and stood in the curtains by myself, close to tears. Then I felt an arm around my shoulder. It was Billy Graham. He had seen my disappointment and came over to encourage me.

"Leighton," he said, "I believe God has given you a burden to see people come to Christ. If you stay humble I believe God will use you. I am going to pray for you."

That arm around the shoulder has stayed with me as have those words of encouragement across the years, as I have passed on to other younger leaders what I received.

That night Billy recommended I consider attending Wheaton College. Neither of us realized that was where I would meet and fall in love with his sister. Jeanie and I were married while I was in seminary, and after graduation he invited me to join his crusade team for a year—which stretched into thirty years of worldwide ministry, longer probably than he intended!

During those years he was a mentor to me, not so much in a close-up relationship, as in the example he set, and the doors he opened. Often he would invite me to sit in on a private luncheon with some church or civic leaders, and I saw how he would graciously weave faith into the conversation. He also trusted me with some demanding assignments.

In the fall of 1956 his team were preparing for his first major crusade in New York City in Madison Square Garden the following summer. He called me up to his home in Montreat and said he wanted me to go to

New York City to help prepare the way. I was to be the key contact with pastors and church leaders across the whole metropolitan area, sharing the vision of how the crusade could help their churches in their outreach. I was twenty-four years old, with absolutely no experience in that role. Seminary had not prepared me for such a task. Looking back I wonder: if I had been him, facing the challenge of his largest crusade to date in the nation's largest city, would I have entrusted such a major responsibility to me?

That "arm around the shoulder" was a symbol of how he so often opened doors for me across thirty years—encouraging me to form a team and evangelize across my native Canada and in other countries, inviting me to bring the message on *The Hour of Decision* broadcast with him every other week, recommending me to speak at special events and serve on some influential boards.

The time also came, in my mature years, when he believed, with changes coming in his organization, it was time for me to leave and begin a new ministry myself. He had opened many doors. Now he closed that one. And the closing of that door was the best thing that could have happened when it did.

A few weeks ago I put my arm around his own shoulder when we visited him at home in the North Carolina mountains. I did so gently, because he is ninety-six, frail, sight and hearing impaired, and sensitive to unexpected touches.

"Billy," I said, as clearly as I could, "I want to thank you for what you meant to me as a boy in Canada, and across the years. Your arm around my shoulder so many years ago I will always remember."

I hoped he could hear me. There was a long pause. Then, quietly he said, "Praise the Lord."

## GIVING UP GREATNESS

The respected chairman of the committee, Anglican bishop A. Jack Dain of Sydney, Australia, was the first chair of the Lausanne Committee for World Evangelization He was a veteran missionary leader in India. Skilled and experienced chair of many global committees. Close friend and confidant of Billy. Executive chair of the Lausanne Congress. Respected around the world. And when he resigned, the seventy-five member committee wondered who would replace him.

A nominating committee asks for names to be considered, and the regional groups all suggest that I succeed Jack as chair. They have asked me to serve in part because they knew me as program chair for the '74 Lausanne Congress. I also suspect it was in part because I came from Canada, a smaller nation known for diplomacy.

But I know I will need help and guidance. And it comes—from the retiring chair, Jack Dain himself.

It's not always easy for an older leader to pass over the reins. In Jack's case it was more than passing over a position. It was staying on in a lesser role.

Jack Dain was a man of tremendous stature and talent. I think he could have been secretary general of the United Nations. But when he came (as he did for many more years) to the meetings of the Lausanne Committee he virtually became my assistant. He would ring the bell to start the meetings. Bring me a glass of water. Let me know of any problems or disagreements in the group. Run interference as needed. Make suggestions as to procedure (but only when asked). And most of all let me know I had his full confidence, support, and prayers.

In those years I needed to fly often to Australia. The flights arrived about 6 a.m. Jack would always be waiting. He would insist, over my objections, on carrying my suitcase even though he was twenty years older than I.

Jack embodied Jesus' value of the elder serving the younger, and has been a model for my own mentoring in years to come.

He became a father in the Lord to me. He had lovely daughters but no son, and in a sense I became that son, and felt cared for as a father does a son.

A few weeks before he died I flew to his home in the south of England. As I sat by his bed I asked him which of all his ministries across the years meant most to him. Without a pause he said, "Being a pastor to the six hundred clergy in Sydney." When I quoted Jesus' words in John 10 about the "other sheep" which needed to be found, Jack broke in and in a weak voice finished the sentence: "Them also I must bring."

With Jack I felt more than a sheep. I felt like a son. Sometimes in a quandary I still stop, look up, and ask, "Jack, what would you do?" And often think I can I sense what his wise answer would be.

## THREADS FRAYED AND GATHERED

I am on a flight I dread to take, the long haul from North Carolina to Sydney, Australia. I dread it not because of the time and distance involved, but because of the separation from home and family, and a huge hole in my heart.

Two months before our beloved twenty-one-year-old son, Sandy, died during surgery at Duke Medical Center to correct a problem with the electrical system of his heart. His death was totally unexpected, and shattering.

Sandy was not only our oldest son, but also a leader for Christ at his university, with a deep desire to serve the Lord in the years to come. He was full of dreams, and so were the expectations Jeanie and I had for him.

Leaving home for a long trek had always been difficult. But this time was so hard because the wound was fresh and grievous. I did not want to leave home. Yet I had promised to speak at an evangelism outreach on the north side of Sydney and I had to go.

On that flight, halfway between the United States and Australia, I was musing about the future. I realized how many grey hairs there were among the leaders in the Lausanne movement. And I wrote in my journal, "Perhaps the next thing is to bring together the emerging young leaders of the world."

In Sydney I asked my friend Bishop John Reid who he saw as future bishops in his diocese. "I can think of many blokes in their thirties," he said, "but not many in their forties who are leader material."

I had already noticed in my travels a leadership gap apparent in the Christian world. Many key leaders who emerged after World War II, who had founded significant ministries, were in their sixties and coming toward the close of their roles. At the same time I had met a number of young leaders in their thirties who had fresh new visions. Between those generations it seemed were many managers, but not many leaders.

For the last two years Jeanie and I had sensed that there might be a change in the direction of my ministry. We had begun a memorial fund after Sandy's death providing educational scholarships to help other young men and women prepare to run their race for Christ. In our hearts we had a desire for other sons and daughters, not to replace Sandy, but to pursue their own callings. And we were praying for clarity in our own calling.

## A NEW THING SPRINGS FORTH

The threads of the new calling were coming together. The loss of a son, leading to a desire to nurture other young men and women. The emerging generation of young leaders around the world. The memory of that arm around the shoulder so many years before. All these were coming together in the forming of a new ministry.

"Don't despise the day of small beginnings" wrote the prophet Zechariah. Leighton Ford Ministries certainly began small. For years I had been speaking to very large crowds. We had a fairly sizeable support and ministry team. And there had been a fair amount of publicity.

At LFM's launch in 1989, there was only myself, a small board and a few advisors, and a handful of prayer supporters.

*Christianity Today* raised the question of what I was now doing and described the new ministry as a transition "from mass evangelist to soul friend."[1] It was in many ways like my former calling, but more personal. It was definitely up close, rather than at a distance. And it was certainly on a smaller scale.

In prayer and silent listening, I sensed strongly that God was saying, "If you want to make a difference, it will happen not through multiplying programs but by investing in people." I wrote that sentence in a notebook that I have kept ever since.

Below I wrote a list of men and women who came to mind, young leaders with potential and a heart for others and for the Lord. Remembering that the missionary leader Oswald Sanders kept a list of "blokes to watch" this became what I called my "GGTW" list—guys and gals to watch.

They came from half a dozen countries and a variety of ministries. I began to pray for them. Called them from time to time. Invited some of them to Charlotte for a day or two of conversation. Took them along on my ministry travels. Eventually some of them and others became part of our first mentoring group—our "Point Group." A few years later I invited a second mentoring group.

The pattern of these connecting groups has been very simple. Once a year we gather for a retreat. For some years we met near where each one lives and ministers, more recently each year in the North Carolina mountains.

Early on I invited some outside person to lecture. But soon we found the most valuable time is simply to be together. Each day we begin with

---

1. Winner, "From Mass Evangelist to Soul Friend."

simple worship. In the mornings each has extended time to share where they are in their lives and ministries. We gather around each other in a circle of prayer. In the afternoons we walk, or run, or rest, or have fun or simply relax together. In the evenings, after a long, relaxed dinner, there is time to talk about whatever is on our minds and in our hearts.

These retreats are a priority for each member. Each one understands that they are to make their participation as serious a priority as they would if they were the main speaker for the week.

We have been meeting annually now for many years. A few have dropped out. Some have been added. One woman came through serious cancer, another man lost a son through addictions, a third died with lung cancer after years of effective ministry as a pastor in Australia.

Many of them have moved into significant national and international leadership roles. Others have faithfully ministered in the same location for many years. Some have faced deep disappointments and seen dreams dashed. Yet through all of this the sense of community has been profound and blessed.

Leaders need safe times, safe places, and safe people to keep going for the long-run.

A leadership development specialist asked, "Can you put what you want to accomplish in one sentence?"

I was stumped for a moment. Then these words came, and I spoke them out loud: "Yes, we want to help young leaders to lead more *like* Jesus, and more *to* Jesus."

I had been writing a book on Jesus as a leader, and had been reading and rereading Mark's Gospel, noting the marks of Jesus' leadership.[2] Many Christian "leadership" books, it seemed, were largely adapted from secular models—good ones, but not singularly based on Jesus' own leadership: the leadership of a son, a servant—and a shepherd-maker.

We would aim to center on Jesus—through the Word and the Spirit helping young leaders worldwide to lead *to* Jesus (in evangelism), *like* Jesus (in character), and *for* Jesus (in motive.)

We began to develop a personalized leadership development program, which would focus both on the character and competence of ministry leaders—a calling to be kingdom-seekers and not empire-builders.

We named it the Arrow Leadership Program. The arrow image had come to me when I was speaking at Duke Divinity School chapel and was

2. Ford, *Transforming Leadership*.

asked how I had seen Billy Graham change across the years. An arrow came to mind. "Billy Graham has been like an arrowhead," I responded, "sharp at the point as the gospel is always at the forefront in his preaching. He has also grown broader like an arrowhead at its base, as he understands the implications of the gospel for issues of poverty and nuclear weapons, and like the shaft of an arrow growing deeper in the Lord."

The Arrow Leadership Program continues internationally under its own auspices, still aiming to help younger leaders become "sharp arrows" (Isa 49:2) in the Lord's hand—sharp in vision, broad in understanding, and deep in God.[3]

At the Arrow sessions I and others had been teaching about leadership, evangelism, communication. But increasingly much of my own time was spent in long walks and talks with young leaders, listening deeply to their desires and longings, the hopes and hurts of their hearts.

While they were grateful for the teachings, I sensed that most of all they longed for an older person who would walk with them, without having a particular agenda to impose, and help them to discern what God was saying to them.

Together we were experiencing "holy listening," what across years of Christian tradition has been called "spiritual direction." It was a term not very familiar then in many evangelical circles, but that now has become much more widely understood and practiced.

Spiritual mentoring is not quite the same as what is often called "discipling," nor the same as coaching, counseling, or teaching. All of these are important elements in leadership development, and a helpful part of mentoring. The focus of spiritual mentoring, however, is to help people to pay attention to what God is doing in their lives, and to respond. It is not "directing" others in the sense of imposing an agenda on them and telling them what to do. Rather it is the companionship of a friend, who listens deeply, who may point out what God is doing and help them to discern God's agenda.

Not only do we have the example of Jesus' own mentoring, but there is a critical need for leaders in ministry today, with all the pressures they face.

Lon Allison, one of our first Point Groupers, posed a provocative question: "What do you think is the number one value of evangelical leaders in the U.S.?"

"What do you think?" I responded.

3  See www.arrowleadership.org.

"Frenzied busyness," he answered. "Based on what leaders talk about when we get together. Everyone is talking or complaining about how busy they are. And if that's what we talk most about it must be what we value most!"

It was a sobering observation. Whether or not it's a "value," I have no doubt that most leaders are not only overbusy, but lead distracted lives in a busy world. Not only are leaders hassled by the external pressures of a busy world, and the expectations of others, but they also live with the internal pressures of dealing with the issues of their own hearts.

I often quote to younger leaders (and some older ones too) an unusual definition of leadership by the educator Parker Palmer: "A leader is a person who has an unusual degree or power to project on other people his or her shadow, or his or her light."[4] They usually respond with a nod and a smile—or a grimace. We can easily think of leaders who are light-projectors and others who spread darkness, but in each of us there are places where light shines, and unrecognized shadow places that need to be brought into the light.

In the midst of these pressures, from without and within, where can leaders go for safe places and times of renewal? Where can they find an older and hopefully wiser person willing to give them time, listen to their hearts, share their hurts, and help them to discern God's agenda for them? That is the question that leads to the need for spiritual companionship and mentoring.

## ORIGINALS, NOT COPIES

I am sitting with my young friend Ken in his car outside Tenth Avenue Church in Vancouver where he has just accepted a call to serve as pastor.

We have known each other now for years, since he was a Wheaton College student and heard me speak and hoped we could some time meet. We did connect when he was student body president at Gordon-Conwell Seminary and I was a trustee. He offered then to drive me to visit some friends, a drive that took several hours. As he drove I leaned back and asked him to tell me his story.

I was very impressed and put him on my "GGTW" list and invited him to join our first Arrow cohort, of which he was the youngest. I did watch him—I observed his heart for God and others, his keen mind and ability

4. Palmer, "Leading from Within," 24–25.

to interact with the material. As a Japanese-Canadian Ken was somewhat reserved, yet well able to relate to the others. In him I saw both a genuine humility, and a clear calling to serve Christ and the gospel.

Ken has reminded me often of that day we sat outside Tenth Church. He had finished seminary, served in a church plant, then felt God had called him back to his native Canada, not sure for what or where. As he walked on the beach one day, seeking direction, the words "Tenth Church" came to mind. He was totally surprised. Tenth was a historic old church, once the flagship of its denomination, but had gone through years of decline. They had had twenty some pastors in twenty some years! A remnant of older people were holding on but it was near to closing.

"I couldn't believe they would want me, in my early thirties, to be their pastor," Ken told me. "But they have called me. And, frankly, I am really anxious. I'm not sure I'm up to it."

After he had poured out his concerns, Ken remembers what I said to him.

"Ken, remember God is an artist. He doesn't do copies. He does originals. And if you are called here God will do something new through you."

And that is what God has done. Through the leadership of Ken and others Tenth Church has made a powerful impact in that very diverse and secular city. The congregation has grown and become diverse ethnically and generationally. Worship is fresh. Preaching is strong. New people have come as a few have left. The church has been recognized with a national award for service to the city. A pimp in the park told a woman in trouble, "Go to Tenth Church. They help people there."

I share Ken's story because I am so thankful for the privilege of helping men and women like him. I could write of many others. I count him, as I do them, not as a "mentoring success" but as a gift from God to his church and the Kingdom. I have watched his growth as a person, a husband to Sakiko and father to Joey, a preacher, author, and friend. He calls me often just to see how I am doing. He is truly a son in the Lord, an arrow in a full quiver.

At its best, spiritual mentoring is a long-term companionship in Christ. As someone has said, a spiritual director remembers our own song when we have forgotten it.

# BIBLIOGRAPHY

Ford, Leighton. *Transforming Leadership: Jesus' Way of Creating Vision, Shaping Values, and Empowering Change.* Downers Grove, IL: InterVarsity, 1991.

Palmer, Parker J. "Leading from Within: Out of Shadow, into the Light." In *Spirit at Work: Discovering the Spirituality in Leadership*, ed. Jay Conger et al., 19–40. San Francisco: Jossey-Bass, 1994.

Winner, Lauren F. "From Mass Evangelist to Soul Friend." *Christianity Today*, October 2, 2000, http://www.christianitytoday.com/ct/2000/october2/7.56.html.

*Chapter 8*

# Many Hands Make Light Work

JASON BYASSEE

I'VE ALWAYS LOVED THE German word for the director of a doctoral dissertation. Such a person is one's *Doktorvater*, literally, a "doctor father." It suggests a combination of expertise and affection, authority and tenderness.

But of course it doesn't always work out correctly, if a story I heard once from Jürgen Moltmann is any indication. He told a small group during a visit to Duke of an experience that he and Eberhard Jüngel and Wolfhart Pannenberg each had. Their great *Doktorvater*, Karl Barth, had come to each of them and anointed him as his successor. To have the greatest Protestant theologian of the twentieth century lay hands on you and ordain you his spiritual heir must have been heady stuff. Each would prove worthy of it—turning in absolutely brilliant theological careers. But each man had the same subsequent experience: Barth took it back. He came back to each of them and revoked his fatherly blessing. He'd observed their work for some time and decided he was not worthy of such anointing. I can't imagine a word of rebuke from such an authority as Barth—let alone his wiping away of the oil of anointing that once shone so proudly on the forehead.

My own *Doktorvater* was Reinhard Hütter, a systematician of some renown who was immeasurably kind to me. I've always felt a slight kinship with Barth, since Alasdair Heron was Reinhard's advisor, and Heron's

*Doktorvater* was the Swiss great himself. Hütter stepped into my program after an unexpected series of events left me without an advisor. He knew enough about Augustine to direct competently and his advice made my work better. But his personal encouragement meant more still. I remember fumbling for words to tell him I'd decided to serve as a student pastor while writing the dissertation. I knew he likely wouldn't approve for fear that I wouldn't finish the degree, but I needed the money (plus the Jesus bit and all). But Dr. Hütter corrected me, with a slight but approving smile, "It's a calling." He never revoked his blessing. The day I defended the dissertation (see! I finished!), Hütter extended his hand to me: "Congratulations, *Dr. Byassee*," he said. "Now you must call me 'Reinhard.'" We were now no longer teacher and pupil, but peers.

We'd long been friends of a sort, without calling it that. For a mentoring relationship has to be voluntary, as friendship must be chosen rather than imposed. One person will not seek out wisdom from another without a mutual appreciation. But affection or even love are not enough. The mentor has to have something to teach—some authority and expertise that the mentee lacks and seeks. Affection and expertise are a lot, but also not enough. There has to be a sense of a shared adventure between the two. In my case with Reinhard we were both about the joyous task of inquiring into the mind of God and learning how to elucidate that mind for others. Finally the mentor and mentee have to be fellow travelers—in our case, Christians. I don't remember praying with Reinhard, and we rarely worshiped together. He later became Roman Catholic in a way that leaves him with little dialogue space with the sort of Protestant I am; I went into journalism and more popular theology, which are not fields in which he has deep interest. But even after these departures, he came to hear me preach in Duke Chapel on Trinity Sunday. The sort of conservative Catholic that Reinhard is doesn't leave him hungry for homiletical tidbits from an ecumenical, generically Protestant campus chapel. But afterwards he again blessed me. With another shake of the hand he said, simply, "You have spoken truly. And well." I love that man.

This essay will be both patristic and autobiographical. I want to talk about mentoring in the church fathers using Edward Smither's book *Augustine as Mentor*.[1] And I want to talk about the role of mentors in my life. I've had more than my fair share, and anything I know about this holy and difficult work I know through these relationships. I'll reflect some on my

---

1. Smither, *Augustine as Mentor.*

middling efforts to mentor others. And, I can't promise I won't use some exegesis of popular movies on the way. For as much as Reinhard taught me about being a human being, his way of doing theology without touching down in biography or popular culture didn't really take root in me. As a good mentor he gave me everything he had, and then let me be me.

It is ironic and painful that Christianity has become so individualistic in western Protestant culture ("me and my personal relationship with Jesus"). For there is no moment in the Christian story that doesn't involve mentoring. Perhaps God could have created and saved us with no need for relationship. But God did not. God spent patient centuries with his people Israel in intimate relationship and still does. God in flesh in Jesus spent years in intimate, painstaking relationship with handpicked disciples who all denied and fled from him at the end. If God is a mentor, either mentoring is not God's best gift, or God has a knack for choosing especially unresponsive mentees. Jesus' resurrection and the Gift of the Spirit at Pentecost show that our failures as disciples are not the end. As Sam Wells's essay in this volume makes clear, God's patience with us as a mentor is fathomless. God almighty chooses to be dependent on us, and vulnerable toward such frail creatures as us, to do his kingdom's advance work in the world. There has to have been a more efficient way to orchestrate salvation than this. But God didn't take it

After the generation of the apostles, the era of the church fathers sees this motif of mentorship deepen. Smither narrates mentorship as something bound up with salvation itself: a mentor coaches disciples toward the fullness of each of their maturity in Christ.[2] Mentoring necessarily assumes a hierarchy. The mentee approaches the mentor out of a desire to learn something the one has that the other does not. The disciple likely doesn't know fully what that is. It is not mere information or data, it is formation, a deepening of a way of life, steeping in a Wisdom that neither possesses in full but both want more deeply. In Smither's words, the mentor has to be a Christian first: one who has progressed a little farther down the way of discipleship. But as Israel's wandering in the wilderness shows, that way can be circuitous indeed. "For you I am a bishop," Augustine told his congregation in one sermon. "With you I am a Christian."[3] Mentoring *works* on this account because the mentor is vastly inadequate and incomplete.

2. Ibid., 12–13.

3. Ibid., 16.

We don't simply copy mentors. We also differentiate ourselves between them, or in my case one of them from the other. Take Bishop Will Willimon and Pastor James Howell, both of whom I've treasured as mentors for more than twenty years, and both of whom have fine essays in this volume. They've accomplished more than most ministers would in twenty lifetimes: more than sixty books and a million copies sold for Will; thousands of church members added at Davidson Methodist and now Myers Park Methodist and a city influenced in Charlotte for James. They are, for my money, the two best preachers living (granted, I could be a tad biased). But I especially notice the way they posture themselves in sermons quite differently. Willimon almost never uses personal examples. His own experience of discipleship is barely there as he preaches. James rarely preaches without a personal example. His gospel is constantly steeped in his own experience. Testimony is a key Methodist practice. We bear witness to the way grace has reshaped our lives and we bear witness to that to others. So James comes by his practice of testimony honestly. But Will has his reasons for not running everything through his own life. He's learned from Barth that the gospel is vastly bigger than the petty souls we stuff it into. And it's true whether he feels it or believes it or not at the moment. He worries that Methodism's failing has been to reduce a cosmic story of a God out of our control to a meager chaplain to my personal wants and needs. Which is right? I'm constantly wondering that as I read and listen to and spend time with these two. I think I tend to think like Will's approach in principle, and figure the gospel doesn't have to pass through me to get to the church. And yet practically I act like James. My own story is the readiest set of examples I have (perhaps a reason to use it less). And I found in ministry that the more I used my own stories the more they warmed up not just to me, but to the gospel we preach. All three of us are on the way, not tragically incomplete, but working out our salvation with fear and trembling, full of hope that God will bring his work in us to completion (to use language more pious than we tend to use when together). And I'm struck that for these differences in shades of emphasis, both mentors have the joy of someone about a task much bigger than himself. A mentor has to be up front about continuing struggles—that's where we mentees learn the best. And there is delight in being inadequate to the task. As Augustine puts it to his church, "I feed you on what I am fed on myself . . . I set food before you from the pantry which I too live on."[4]

4. Ibid., 128.

You have to be a human being with a soul first. Mentoring is a species of friendship. And friendship always leaves you vulnerable. Either party can betray. St. Ambrose, Augustine's own mentor, wrote to a colleague that he sent letters partly because they helped him feel less lonely, and closer to his friend.[5] Elsewhere Ambrose wrote these touching words: "Blush not to ask questions of your father."[6] He wanted to have his life explored, poked around in, examined, learned from. Not mechanically. There is a soul in there. And of course that openness makes rejection and pain possible. Just ask Jesus. This is all the more poignant when we remember Ambrose's role in Augustine's life. His eloquent preaching dragged Augustine out of disinterest while he was in the imperial capital of Milan making a name for himself and avoiding the Church Catholic. Ambrose's eloquence and brilliance as bishop of Milan brought Augustine to church, and gave him better wisdom on the Old Testament than he ever got from other Catholics or from the Manichean sect he'd joined. He signed up for baptism and was likely instructed by Ambrose. But then in a famous scene in *Confessions* Augustine sought Ambrose's company. But Ambrose seems to have ignored him. Augustine reports being amazed that Ambrose could read without speaking aloud (truly a gift when there are no spaces between the words—ancient writing materials were expensive). But he got no time with him. Perhaps Ambrose was cognizant that Augustine had gotten his job via his Manichean connections. Whatever the reason, he remained cool toward him. Augustine here opened himself up and Ambrose refused to reciprocate. I remember with gratitude Willimon's tenderness in his call to me when his own South Carolina Annual Conference, which had long held him at arm's length, nominated him to be a bishop. "They picked *me!*" he said with the vulnerability of an eighth grader. You'd think he wouldn't have needed such approval. But you'd be wrong. We all need such approval.

Now, we are all blessedly finite creatures. We only have time and energy for so many relationships and so cannot be relationally omnivorous. But I wonder about the role of pain in mentoring. Bill Gattis, longtime preacher at University Methodist in Chapel Hill, likes to quote a Sufi mystic on this. A would-be disciple approaches with an expression of love, and the teacher asks if the student knows what hurts him. No, he says. "How can you claim to love me if you don't know my pain?" My learning curve has always been steeper when mentors have opened up their pain to me. They're

5. Ibid., 78.

6. Ambrose, *Letter* 27 (to Irenaeus), quoted in Smither, *Augustine as Mentor*, 85.

not maudlin or showy about it. They just make clear their pain motivates them in some way. And of course they do this knowing opening themselves up could make for greater pain. The same is true for me. I'm wondering what I should do with the pain I've been saddled with. And opening myself up could make for more of it. It sometimes has. And it's worth it.

Often these issues of pain have to do with our families, especially our parents. I shouldn't speak for my friends, but I'm sure I wouldn't be as wrapped up in church were it not for a painful relationship with my mother. I love the ancient church's language about the church as our mother. And I've been aware that I seek God partly out of a sense of lack in my relationship to my own parents. An impolite challenger might say religion is always doing this—foisting our needs on the sky and feigning divine receptivity. And as a Barthian I worry about reducing God to the cramped contours of my shabby heart. Yet the gospel is at least about repair (at most it's about a new creation vastly greater than, but including, the old). Something precious has been ruined, and some One powerful is in the restoration business. The church has often been a surrogate family for me in place of a ruined one. It's not without its own flaws God knows! It can harm as well as heal. And yet the church and my mentors specifically have noticed me, encouraged me, spoken to my fears. More basically they've been there. Answered calls, sent texts and timely notes, convinced me I could do things I didn't think I could. They've also been gracious with my failures. These are things parents do. Willimon asked me to help him with a project once that I wasn't up to. He never mentioned my failure to deliver again, but passed over it in graceful silence. James disagreed with me once on a key move in my life (well, more than once, and he hasn't been wrong yet). I went after him, attacked him, yelled at him. He backed down and supported me. But when it came unglued he never said "I told you so." He moved in with comfort and grace. These two have been friends before anything else, and they've been kind more than anything else. And there is a strange alchemy of hurt and need for healing, vulnerability and openness to rejection, the making of new relationships and the possibility of restoration all involved in mentoring. Augustine prays to God about Ambrose in *Confessions*, "Unknowingly I was led by you to him, so that through him I might be led knowingly to you."[7]

One key mentor of sorts in *Confessions* is Marius Victorinus, a great philosopher renowned in ancient Rome who became a Christian. The

---

7. Augustine, *Confessions* 5.13.23, quoted in Smither, *Augustine as Mentor*, 103.

bishops were willing to let him make his profession of faith privately so as not to embarrass him. But he insisted on his praise of God ringing out as confidently as his former atheism had done. His example as a great intellect boldly professing faith encouraged Augustine to do the same. But before this conversion, Marius had teased others about their insistence that he profess his faith in church. He already believed. He was a Christian "in his heart." Is God confined to the four walls of a building? In a sense, yes. God is not so confined by nature. But God freely chooses confinement by electing Israel, being fleshed through Mary, choosing forever to be saddled with the church.

I'm struck by how James and Will have helped me make sense of the four walls of United Methodism. I came to the UMC with a sneer, born of evangelical faith and a confidence I was right about the contours of the gospel (still have that honestly). And as far as I could tell the UMC didn't much care about faithfulness to scripture and tradition. I saw bishops mock orthodoxy, pastors dodge it. Churches haven't so much raged into obsolescence as they have snored into it. How can we make something so magnificent as God and the gospel into an invitation for a nap?! We've done it, and being boring is a worse sin than being a heretic. So why am I here? Why am I yoked to Methodism in a way that's unalterable? Because of these two mentors. James was unsure at first: "You don't sound *mainline* to me," he said in our first-ever conversation. He was right—I was a leader in InterVarsity, worshiping at PCA churches, and considering evangelical seminaries. But I was committed not to reduce the gospel to partisan politics, as I often saw done in the evangelical world. I'd grown up in hyper-liberal Chapel Hill and hated that my friends could dodge Jesus by pointing out his friends seemed to love the Republican Party more than the gospel. My being outspoken in the other political direction led to Christian friends worrying, praying for me, and occasionally distancing themselves (and, honestly, not many of my pagan friends noticing or caring). I noticed that in the evangelical world I couldn't figure out who my friends and enemies *were*. At least in the mainline I could tell where the battle lines were. I'd be a conservative in a liberal context. And I was right to choose this side—some of my more conservative friends who've become pastors have been charged with heresy in some ridiculous semi-formal sense.

James and Will helped me learn to love these four walls—of United Methodism. They modeled faithful ministry to me. I withdrew from the evangelical world and went to Davidson Methodist because that was where the good preaching was going on. James was learned without being showy. He was captivating rhetorically precisely because he was captivated by God. He wanted our hearts converted toward Jesus and wanted our souls in love with Jesus' beloved poor. He was good, and I wanted more. So too Willimon when I arrived at Duke Divinity as a student and he was Dean of the Chapel. He took an interest in me, spent time with me, patiently answered stupid questions about abortion and infant baptism (important topics—but my approach was not brilliant!). And more importantly he preached beautifully. He wrote like an angel. He seemed to be having fun. He was a model faculty member, reading colleagues' work and commenting with enthusiasm when he could have cocooned himself in his own projects. These two work to make the gospel believable in all its magnificence in a world that's usually disinterested or actively opposed and a church rarely worthy of the name. They showed me what kind of evangelical I am. And that the United Methodist Church, for all its ridiculous flaws, is the beloved bride of Christ. There is no "better" church to retreat to, not least because if we go we take all our flaws with us. It's an Augustinian point—there is no sinless church. Just this batch of hapless losers trying to stumble around after Jesus. Which is all there's ever been in the first place.

Mentoring can be both hierarchical and gracious. I would not have sought out James or Will if they weren't vastly better than I. Neither has ever been an official supervisor, which has probably helped (perhaps that's just my modernist self talking, preferring to be a free agent than to be prodded toward holiness). But they have had the more informal "power" to bless or withhold blessing. The ancient church had more resources to produce "holy fear" in disciples. The bishop had to be loved and honored as a representative of God in his person. This makes me uncomfortable honestly. Our age is right I think to mistrust authority, we've seen it so vastly misused. But without hierarchy of a sort there is nothing to learn and no way to grow. With these two the hierarchy has been a chosen one, more a friendship than one with the possibility of coercion. But the hierarchy is clear nonetheless. I love and admire them and want their approbation and love in return.

At Boone Methodist I was privileged to get to practice being the mentor for four years. We hired a tremendously gifted young African-American pastor. Brandon Wrencher has made me look good at every turn. He was also, embarrassingly, our church's first black preacher ever (that in 2013). When I hired him, I asked Willimon for advice. "Be hard on him," he said. Liberal Protestant church leaders tend to hire minorities and then treat them with kid gloves, convinced if we exercise any power it'll be implicitly or (horror of horrors) explicitly racist. But Brandon wanted to work for me because he wanted to get better, and saw in me some resources to help him do this. It would have been no gift to him to chortle nervously over every imperfection and pass it off for fear of racism. It'd have been patronizing. In short, it'd have been racist itself. There is no more unforgivable sin among mainline Protestants than committing an -ism. And tiptoeing as though on thin ice is no way to avoid it. I probably wasn't as intentionally hard on Brandon as he deserved. But my failures were hard on him. He had to step in and do work he didn't know how to do because I was no good at it. And it made him better. As I leave after some years together I see he doesn't need me anymore, or at least not as badly. I need him though, and I think he needs me, as a friend. I love him and delight in his success and will continue to.

This mutual need stands out over against popular culture's depiction of mentoring. There is still a pride of place in Hollywood for the sports or military leader who is basically a tiny dictator. Movies depict drill sergeants yelling at trainees, in their face, abusing them to get the best out of them. Actual military trainers say this is less effective today. For decades in the US, sports coaches took their lead from the military, which makes sense since many of our early great coaches had been military men. They also say this is less effective now. But don't tell Hollywood. One Oscar winner recently was *Whiplash*, about a music teacher who abuses his star pupil in order to get the best out of him. The boy not only bleeds and immorally elbows others out of his way—he is actually lucky to live. The concluding scene has the disgraced former teacher set the boy up to fail one more time in public. He instead turns in a virtuoso performance that earns an appreciative nod. There's the myth once again—the teacher may seem to be mean, but it's only to get the best out of you.

By contrast, think of other Hollywood portrayals of mentorship that are so transcendent it's hard to unthink them. The *Lord of the Rings* movies work partly because Ian McKellen *becomes* Gandalf. Who doesn't want a powerful sage who can race to our rescue, spout koans worth remembering, and will go to the depths of hell for us? I like to refer to Leighton Ford, another mentor a generation older than James and Will (and author of another excellent essay in this book), as "my Gandalf." And he has raced to my rescue multiple times. His powers as a wizard are less supernatural than Mithrandir's (at least for now). A generation before in Hollywood we had

Alec Guinness's Obi-Wan Kenobi (is the English accent required?! Goodness). Kenobi taught Luke Skywalker everything he knew and then grew more powerful in death, not less. He can come to the rescue too. Strikingly these mythic figures often do not come to the rescue of their mentees at quite the time or in precisely the way Frodo or Luke want. They give them space to fail and even to suffer. But theirs is a power and a hope that is supernatural. And to point out the obvious, it is *good*. "Luke! Don't give in to hate. That leads to the dark side," Obi-Wan councils Luke. "Don't be so quick to dole out death and judgment," Gandalf rightly corrects Frodo.

Lest we make mentoring seem a same-gender-only club, we should point out Lady Galadriel has her mentoring power in *LOTR*, and as the temporally last *Star Wars* film closes before this book comes out, Princess Leia is showing remarkable promise with the force. I wish Ellen Davis had been present at Duke for longer than the time necessary to serve on my doctoral committee. Just to make amends I followed her to the ends of the earth. She's deeply interested in what was then southern Sudan, what is now South Sudan, and I traveled there with her and a group in 2009 simply because she was interested. And I wasn't disappointed. Many of her former students from Virginia Theological Seminary are Sudanese, including significant prelates in the Episcopal Church of Sudan (ECS). Archbishop Daniel Deng Bul is primate of that church, and a former student. One day while we were there he rose in his cathedral in front of a thousand or so worshipers and asked Ellen, a lay person, to give the benediction. He said that he could have easily hated his Muslim neighbors. People do terrible things in civil wars and memories are long. But partly with Ellen's teaching he had learned instead to love the sons and daughters of Ishmael. Ellen accepted his invitation. She raised her hands such that she looked even more like a matriarch in Israel than usual. And I remember her beginning the benediction in Arabic. She insists she did not, that she could have said no more than As-Salaam Alaikum (it's not surprising that I promote her linguistic powers of blessing in my memory). Then she blessed us with the Aaronic blessing in Hebrew. And then in English. She united in her person the languages with which divided peoples pray, oppose one another, and love. I'd follow her to the ends of the earth again.

There is a kind of otherworldly power to our mentors. I wish it were actually miraculous, and touching the hem of their garment would actually bring instant healing. But I do find that I want to be near them partly because their mere presence seems palpably holy. I'm not naïve—I've already made clear these men and women are up front about their faults. But just being with them does more than make me feel better. It makes me long for holiness too. I want to be a better man when I'm with them. And that's a power beyond the normal course of things in our world. It's why mentors can indeed abuse or mistreat. And it's why they can make us better than we are. Which is about the best power a human being can have, in this or any universe.

Augustine seems to have had a more than ordinary desire to be with others. He was a social creature, and he was nudged by and nudged his friends toward God. His own conversion was entangled with others'. And more importantly so was his practice of leadership. One major contribution as a bishop was to bring the habits of the monastery into the diocese.[8] Between his conversion and his ordination he spent his time in a sort of holy leisure, conversing with other Christian friends (and his mother and son) about philosophical topics, seeking to grow in wisdom. In our terms, he went to seminary. But then he was taken by force and ordained against his will. Not a practice he would later promote, but it was done. Would he give up those meaty friendships and get on with the administrative busywork? No. He brought his way of being friends into the work of a bishop. It was different now—a sort of holy burden rather than holy leisure. He lived together with others. They prepared food together and Augustine always had extra places set at his table. Bishops were commanded to be hospitable not less than the monks by whom Augustine had been inspired. His biographer Possidius reports that Augustine was more delighted by conversation with others at table than he was by food and drink.[9] And Augustine kept a prerogative over them that I love. If anyone swore an oath at his table, that one was docked one drink of his allotment of wine![10] This is the perfect penalty. The only gift Augustine had to give was himself; the only punishment a slight reduction in the joy of being together.

The friends invited to live with him rose with him to pray. They concluded the day with prayer. They studied scripture together. They also conducted dialogues. This was partly inspired by the philosophers they studied, but it was also inspired by the gospel. Jesus taught and discussed with his friends. And the bishop may have stood for Jesus in his person, but

---

8 Smither, *Augustine as Mentor*, 155, citing Lawless, *Augustine of Hippo and His Monastic Rule*.

9 Smither, *Augustine as Mentor*, 153.

10. Ibid., 154.

he was not above reproach, disagreement, correction. Augustine had a rich interpersonal life. He could not approach this God without these people; nor these people without this God. The gospel is a matter of love after all. It cannot be passed on without blood and tears and joy.

Once a mentee had passed through the training ground of Augustine's own house, he equipped them and set them loose. He often coauthored letters with them, giving them opportunities to write. He invited them to lead with him, especially in areas where Augustine himself was weak. Smither points out especially that Augustine did not feel strong in administration. His mentee Eraclius was. So Augustine turned to his expertise and eventually had him named his successor. Augustine knew that Punic-speaking areas needed the gospel in their language, which he did not speak. So he sent his disciples with those gifts to those areas. Sometimes these produced great effect; sometimes they were failures. But Augustine did not keep his students close forever. He sent them away. They could succeed or fail on their own terms. And, strikingly, Augustine's pupils did not become great writers or preachers.[11] We do not all have the gifts we wish we did, or that our mentors wish we would. The goods we pursue together as mentor and mentee are goods of the kingdom that God will bring to fruition in God's own mysterious time and way. But his mentees did not fail because Augustine did not give them everything he had. He shared table and house with them. He wrote his books and treatises for them, largely in response to their pastoral crises, seeking to equip them for ministry. And even though he hated travel he would go far to be with them, bless them, equip them anew. Possidius was aware that Augustine was an epochal intellect in the church. He still wrote this,

> I believe, however, that they profited even more who were able to hear him speaking in church and see him there present, especially if they were familiar with his manner of life among his fellow human beings.[12]

Augustine's mentees may have failed, as he often did. But these failures did not happen because he withdrew or withheld himself from them. He shared himself fully, to the end. I often detect in myself a reticence to mentor. This is not out of a holy awareness of my sin or pride. It is a fear that I'll be found out, caught as a fraud, denounced as a pretender. If I just pull

---

11. Ibid., 257.

12. Possidius, *Life of Augustine* 31.9, quoted in Smither, *Augustine as Mentor*, 119.

the curtain a little tighter maybe they'll never know. I'm struck that those who've mentored me, and those I've successfully mentored, have no such illusion. They see my flaws clearer than I do. And they require no curtain. At their best they yank it away. Augustine had no curtain. He and his disciples pursued life together. They shared work. And he sent them on their way, to do what they could, and he could not, with his frail best. I'm impressed that the most important thing my mentors have done with and for me is just to spend time with me. Much of it is silly time. We laugh and drink and carry on in ways that may have drawn Augustine's disapproval. We gossip and joke and encourage. And we settle down into important things—offering correction, grace, our flawed and frail perceptions of one another, our best but still limited insight on what the future holds in each other's career. And we are for one another. I would walk in front of the train for these guys. They would for me. It's the sort of friendship that allows you to see and touch the face of God. It is the gospel—God's mixing himself up in the flesh of our life and mixing us up in one another's. It's tremendously flawed. And it's even more tremendously good.

Christianity is a matter of passing on to others what we have, in turn, received (1 Cor 15:1–11). This passing on only really works in a relationship of love. I wouldn't take something so weighty as a cross, with such a promise of glory as a resurrection, from a stranger or someone I didn't care about, or who didn't care about me. And I'm struck as I take that cross and that promise that it has finger prints all over it—including Augustine's, those of these friends living, those of other friends long dead and more alive than we can imagine. Staggeringly I get to add mine to it on the way to others carrying it as well. The responsibility, the weight of this burden, could hardly be heavier.

Thank God we never carry it alone.

## BIBLIOGRAPHY

Lawless, George. *Augustine of Hippo and His Monastic Rule.* Oxford: Clarendon, 1990.
Smither, Edward L. *Augustine as Mentor: A Model for Preparing Spiritual Leaders.* Nashville: B&H Academic, 2008.

# Chapter 9

# Mentored by the Spirit
## The Practice of Spiritual Direction

## MELANIE L. DOBSON

### DIRECTED BY MARY

The teapot bubbled and sang just after I walked in the front door. The cool dark interior foyer provided respite from the blazing Phoenix, Arizona sun. As my eyes adjusted, I smelled the covers of many books filling the house, and felt comforted. A petite woman with short white hair approached, extending a hand and saying, "Welcome, I'm Mary. I'm so glad you have come." Her face, with wrinkles etched by years of a contented smile, exuded a peace about which I could only dream.

"Would you like a tea?" Somehow, even though the air was melting my car tires outside, the dusty, serene library-like feel inside made hot tea seem just right and proper. "Yes," I replied. While she bustled about with the ease of a grandmother in the kitchen, we covered basic pleasantries. With mugs in our hands, a divine lemon scent wafting from them, she guided me into a living room, lined with bookshelves (there are the pages I smelled!) and to two cozy chairs, with a tiny table in between.

"Why don't we take a moment for silence," she gently said. "I like to use a word, a sacred word like 'hope,' 'love,' 'joy' to come back to when my mind wanders—which it usually wanders," she said with a grin. "Let's settle in, and allow God to speak to us."

I obediently followed her, closing my eyes and attempting to arrange my face into the tranquility that hers radiated. Almost immediately, within half a second, my mind felt like it held one hundred dancing monkeys. Three or four swooped around on branches of thought about phone calls, emails, etc. I needed to return. At least a dozen clung to me about my insufficiency as a pastor. A dozen whooped and hollered all the details of the upcoming youth retreat, upcoming sermon, upcoming missions trip . . .

A tinkling tiny bell. Mary called us out of prayer. She continued to emanate serenity. I, on the other hand, must have looked exhausted. She took a deep and satisfied breath. I attempted to do so, too, but it probably sounded more like a wild gasping for air. She asked, "Let's start with you sharing where you are with God right now, however you want to do that." Open-ended question.

I decided for honesty. "I feel worn out trying to work for God. I can't build a youth ministry fast enough for the parents at my church. I work eighty hour weeks and weekends and the work is never done and it never feels good enough." I droned on for a while.

Mary simply listened. She didn't try to correct me or change me or advise me (though I could have benefited from all of that). Mary gave me the freedom and safe space to tell my truth and she offered me the gift of being heard.[1] She created a holy space, allowing me to hear myself narrating my own story. As she did, I could begin to hear how overwhelmed, insecure, and uncertain I was . . . how bereft I felt of God, even as I endlessly busied myself with church work. I so desperately needed this time of holy listening, of someone helping me to see the Spirit at work in my life, when I was feeling too burdened with ministry to pay attention.[2] We arranged that I would come once a month for an hour.

These sessions became an oasis of solace in the sometimes harsh, blazing climate of the first years of ministry. She opened my eyes to the little miracles along my way—a troubled teenager confiding in me, a family's gratitude after a funeral. She nudged me into recognizing that the church member who blessed me out after a sermon might be used by God for my own growth. When I gave more attention to parishioners' emails than my

1. Insight from Sue Monk Kidd.
2. Guenther, *Holy Listening*, 1.

relationship with God, she embodied grace and love. Several months into our spiritual-direction relationship, Mary rejoiced with me when I married.

Mary didn't offer counseling for my problems, or offer therapy. A profoundly wise, married Catholic laywoman (with children and grand-children), she nonetheless didn't attempt pastoral care, nor did she try to be a friend.[3] She provided a healing space of listening with me to God, and caring—her way of being present to me assured me that my life mattered to God and to her. Through the Holy Spirit at work within her, she mentored me in my life of faith. She embodied the definition of spiritual direction: "help given by one Christian to another which enables that person to pay attention to God's personal communication to him or her, to respond to this personally communicating God, to grow in intimacy with this God, and to live out the consequences of the relationship."[4]

At about the same time as I began direction with Mary, I also started in a required covenant group with a mentor for my ordination process in the United Methodist Church. My mentor in this group was deeply formed by spiritual practices and also a wise, older female who had been honed by years in ministry. She was truly wonderful, and a great blessing to me. Yet, there was something about the required nature of this mentorship that made it less enduring to me over the arc of my life than my relationship with my spiritual director. Spiritual directors come as gifts; I had found Mary by asking at the Franciscan Renewal Center in Scottsdale, Arizona (while there on a retreat) for a list of recommended directors. I met with a couple, and quickly discerned that Mary's spirit was the one with which I most resonated. Mary came into my life as a result of prayer, discernment, and gift.[5] My mentor in the ordination process, while also a gift, was as-signed, tasked with an ordination process requirement, and charged with this work for a limited period of time.[6] The Spirit did indeed work through the formality of this procedure, and I learned from my mentor helpful pas-toral practices. Mary's mentoring, however, was more understated, more organic and lasting. My ordination mentor trained me in the life of a min-ister; Mary trained me in a life with God. Her wisdom indelibly formed the way I pray, how I daily meet with the One who made me.

---

3. Jones, *Art of Spiritual Direction*, 20–21.

4. Barry and Connolly, *Practice of Spiritual Direction*, 8.

5. Bakke, *Holy Invitations*, 95–114.

6. Ibid., 29, 31.

Mary embodied holiness to me. She clearly loved the Bible and the Church, and cultivated a fertile prayer life.[7] She was also deeply formed by contemplative prayer. I was drawn to that, having had little to no experience with apophatic spirituality in my Protestant upbringing. Though I didn't really know what it was at the time, Mary taught me centering prayer, the practice of sitting in silence and listening to God, using a sacred word when the mind wanders.[8] Gently, and with great compassion, she told me about finding and coming back to a sacred word, of cultivating a daily twenty-minute morning sit, and then when I got that down, to practice an afternoon twenty minute sit as well.

About six months into our directing relationship, and three months after my wedding, her eyes brimmed with loving concern as I shared of my body falling apart, of lost vision and pain and legs that stopped functioning. Mary didn't try to lessen my terror, or diminish the challenge before me with vacant assurances that everything works to the good for those that love the Lord. Things weren't working to the good; it looked like I was having my first flare of a significant neurological disease at age twenty-seven. She had the wisdom to let me cry, without trying to stop the flow with a hurried offer of Kleenex. Mary held me with a steady, silent presence.

As I journeyed into a new life as a person with a chronic disease, sometimes the most spiritual I'd be in a month was coming and sitting with her and smelling the zest of lemon, and receiving life. In fact, I totally flunked doing centering prayer on my own. Mary was patient while I didn't do the practices she suggested to me. She prayed for me when I had no words and couldn't pray. She simplified, and offered me the Welcoming Prayer as a practice to do between doctor's appointments and church meetings.[9] Mary apprenticed me in my new, unexpected life with illness, teaching me that God accompanied me in my suffering—because she, as a representative of the Spirit, was not afraid to come alongside me in my pain.

7. Nouwen, "Hearing God's Voice and Obeying," 7.

8. Father Thomas Keating has been integral in reviving the practice of contemplative prayer in the Christian tradition, and creating the now global organization Contemplative Outreach. See Keating, *Open Mind, Open Heart*, for an introduction to centering prayer.

9. Mrozowski, www.contemplativeoutreach.org.

## DIRECTED BY STUDY

Eventually, my experience with a chronic neurological condition drove me to leave my wonderful church in Arizona, and go back to school to study questions of suffering, illness, and health in Christian ethics and tradition. Though I tried to keep up with Mary via email, and we did a couple of direction sessions by phone, the distance from Durham, North Carolina, to Tempe, Arizona, stretched long. I eventually lost contact. I grieved the loss of Mary and her presence in my life. I knew I needed another director, but I just didn't have the emotional space to find a new one.

Instead, since I had plunged fully into a life of study, I did a course on spiritual direction, taught by an amazing Catholic sister. I learned more of the art of spiritual direction and practiced it with peers in the course.[10] We learned to welcome silence, to create a safe space, to ask questions like Jesus did: "What do you seek,?" as he did to the disciples of John the Baptist or "What do you want me to do for you?" to blind Bartimaeus.[11] Most importantly, we struggled through practicing being fully present to another, to listen without trying to make a response, to hear another's story without commentary or "fix-its."[12]

In this studious season of life, my husband and I welcomed a baby boy, and nurturing his life, along with participation in a doctoral program, took all I could muster. My son taught me, though, finally to sit and pray. In the wee hours of the morning, when no one was up but Trappist monks and exhausted parents, I fed him milk, and used that sacred, liminal time between night and morning to pray. I was finally beginning to practice centering prayer—directed in this case not by a wise woman—but by the needs of my son. Appropriately named Elijah, he taught me to hear God in the still silence. I so wanted to tell my spiritual director that I was finally, actually doing centering prayer . . . but my emails came back to me.

## DIRECTED BY PAT

Then we moved to Colorado for my husband to start his medical practice. I was writing my dissertation, taking care of a toddler, and after a little while, solo pastoring a small United Methodist church. I was now older,

10. Bakke, *Holy Invitations*, 141, 143.

11. Guenther, *Holy Listening*, 24.

12. Jones, *Art of Spiritual Direction*, 109.

more experienced in ministry, more aware of the essential need of Sabbath and spiritual practices to sustain me. Yet, I felt lonely and isolated in a high Rocky Mountain valley, tucked into a small town about twenty-five minutes downhill from Aspen. I desperately needed a spiritual director. A wonderful retired pastor suggested Pat. "She's been with Father Keating since he began Contemplative Outreach," he said with a smile. "You'll love her."

Love her I did. Pat, mother of ten children, white hair and a rosy face, always laughing wise Catholic laywoman who lives and breathes God's love. I knew immediately that here was one I could trust to guide me in my relationship with God (and as an added "sign" that she was to be my director, she knew Mary!). With a broad and deep contemplative spirit she welcomed me into her home, refused any pay, and ushered me into the presence of God. We began our time with centering prayer—while the cold snowy alpine winter blew outside, we sat on zafu cushions in her upstairs "prayer room"; in the summer we sat on her wide front swing, squinting our eyes under the brilliant, sparkling Colorado sun. She served me hot tea, this time alpine berry from a local tea company. We sipped and talked, and I drank in her wisdom.

Pat had mothered a profoundly disabled child among her brood, who then died in her thirties, just a few years before I met Pat. The spiritual-direction gurus, Barry and Connolly, say that qualified directors believe that God's light overcomes the darkness within us.

> They [good directors] have experienced their own fears and darkness, their own demons, and have also experienced salvation from them. They have experienced God as the one who loves first—the one who loved them when they were dead in their sins—who loves them with all their ambivalence, all their love and hatred, all their lusts, their fears, their selfishness and unselfishness. They have been enabled by such experiences of God to love themselves and to change. Thus, they have an attitude of quiet trust that God will do similar things for others. In other words, they have become less afraid of real people and of the darker sides of real people because they have experienced a God who loves and saves real people like themselves.[13]

Pat's journey through the grief of losing a daughter, her travels with another daughter through a divorce, her experience of all kinds of darkness

---

13. Barry and Connolly, *Practice of Spiritual Direction*, 125.

in her life and the lives of people whom she led on silent retreats, honed her into a person who loved with the ferocity and glory of God. She was completely unafraid of real people and their darker sides.

She was exactly the director I needed as my own marriage unraveled. She was God's presence when I felt abandoned. She sat in the dark tomb of loss with me, unafraid but with profound tenderness. With that quiet trust, she demonstrated to me a God who loves and saves—and who would keep doing that every morning. Somehow, she got me on a weeklong silent retreat at our nearby St. Benedict's (Trappist) Monastery, where she worked, because she trusted the silence would be healing. It was. She listened and asked questions, and helped me to discern my next steps . . . leaving my second beloved church, going with my son back home to North Carolina. She helped me to see that my changing and small life, about which I was so greatly troubled, was part of the great mystery of life known and treasured by God.[14] She reminded me that many lives—Abraham, Sarah, Moses, Esther, Mary, Peter, and many others—followed a different life direction than they had planned or would have chosen, and found God along the way.[15] When the time came for my move, Pat prayed over me, blessed me, and offered a benediction on my unexpected path, assuring me that God would be on my route, too.

## DIRECTED BY GOD

Now I dwell back in the land of the American South, home. I'm pastoring in a large Methodist church. Like with Mary, I emailed a couple of times with Pat, had a few phone conversations, but the distance from Colorado to North Carolina stretches long. I've been blessed to receive direction from a thoughtful and generous United Methodist laywoman. Recently, I've settled in with another wise, Catholic grandmother who sees deeply into the heart of God.

In the meanwhile, I've realized I'm really in the middle. I'm no longer young or inexperienced, yet I don't feel I possess the deep and wide practice and spirit of the directors I've been blessed to have. I will admit that most mornings now find me in centering prayer—not because I'm holy, but because I need that time with God to function. I've finally responded to the Spirit's nudges, and have begun a Spiritual Direction certification program.

14. Underhill, *Spiritual Life*, 95–97.
15. Bakke, *Holy Invitations*, 88.

As a part of that program, I've begun offering spiritual direction to a couple of parishioners. I've got teabags ready in my church office closet, and a tea-kettle awaits in the staff break room, ready to boil. As a directee takes a seat before me, I say, "Welcome. I'm so glad you have come. Would you like a tea? Let's settle in and allow God to speak to us . . ."

## BIBLIOGRAPHY

Bakke, Jeannette. *Holy Invitations*. Grand Rapids: Baker, 2000.

Barry, William A., and William J. Connolly. *The Practice of Spiritual Direction*. New York: Seabury, 1982.

Caussade, Jean-Pierre de. *Sacrament of the Present Moment*. Father de Caussade's Prayer for the Blessed State of Self-Abandonment. Harper One: New York, 1989.

Guenther, Margaret. *Holy Listening: The Art of Spiritual Direction*. Cambridge, MA: Cowley, 1992.

Jones, W. Paul. *The Art of Spiritual Direction: Giving and Receiving Spiritual Guidance*. Nashville: Upper Room, 2002.

Nouwen, Henri J. M. "Hearing God's Voice and Obeying His Word: A Dialogue with Richard Foster and Henri Nouwen." *Leadership Journal* (Winter 1982). http://www.christianitytoday.com/le/1982/winter/hearinggodsvoice.html.

Underhill, Evelyn. *The Spiritual Life*. Wilton, CT: Morehouse Barlow, 1955.

*Chapter 10*

# A Good Work Has Begun in You
## Mentoring College Students for Ministry

CRAIG T. KOCHER

I WOULD NOT BE an ordained minister if influential people in my life who desired the best for me had not encouraged me to explore ministry as my life's vocation. I now understand this network of mentoring relationships as the activity of grace, the explicit and tangible way in which God has been visible in my life, drawing me ever closer to the grain of the kingdom and life in the church.

For the last fifteen years my ordained work has been expressed as a campus minister and chaplain on three different college campuses: Davidson College, Duke University, and the University of Richmond. In those fifteen years I have done my best to mentor young people in their own vocational adventure, and I have encouraged many of them to consider the ordained life as one worth living. This essay is an effort to share some of what I have learned from the mentors in my life, and offer what I have discovered as a mentor to hundreds of college students, some fifty of whom have discerned their own call to professional ministry and are serving Christ creatively and courageously in a variety of ministry settings around the world.

By the time I was a junior at the University of North Carolina I was on the fast track to a career in sports broadcasting. I had a job with the Tar Heel Sports Network broadcasting Carolina Women's basketball and Carolina baseball games, and had traveled to famous venues across the United States as a reporter and play-by-play broadcaster for UNC. It was intoxicating for a sports-obsessed college kid who had grown up in Chapel Hill. At the beginning of my senior year I had a full-time job offer waiting for me after graduation.

My college experience was not limited to sports, however. I was still active in my home church, University United Methodist in Chapel Hill, and was heavily involved in the Wesley Foundation at UNC. While I loved exploring the finer details of the motion offense, I was consumed by theological wonderings and curiosities about God's wider purposes for the world and my life. A trio of beloved pastor mentors, Bill Gattis, Ron Gonia, and Manuel Wortman were unendingly patient and supportive, never force-feeding easy answers to my long-winded questioning, while ever so gently affirming my seeking ways and guiding me towards a more expansive vision of God, church, and kingdom.

By the fall of my senior year I had decided that as much as I loved sports, a life of sports journalism would not fill the deeper craving I felt in my heart and soul. I chose divinity school, and later ordained ministry, and only now in retrospect do I see this as calling, as the subtle movement of the Spirit, guiding me into pastoral work, a way of life I have chosen and one that has chosen me. My life would have been completely different, and profoundly impoverished, without the attentive mentoring of those three pastors and many others to appear over the last twenty years—three of whom, James Howell, Will Willimon, and Sam Wells, have their own essays in this volume. No one in the history of Christianity has benefited from better guides, and these three in particular have filled my life with profound joy and wisdom, beyond what I believe they know. This is an aspect of mentoring I will speak to later in this essay—that mentors are rarely conscious of their influence on the mentee, but rather the mentoring relationship exists as an authentic expression of the character and personality of those involved.

All this is to say, mentoring college students for ordained ministry matters. My life is a testimony to it.

Recent studies affirm what many of us who work on college campuses already know: students are desperate for adults to take an active interest in their lives, and are equally desperate to be engaged in critical questions about the big questions of life: Who am I? What do I believe? Does God exist, and if so what difference does that make? What do I think about marriage and children? What am I supposed to do with my life?

Yet, much of higher education, and wider society, has grown wary of close relationships between older folks and younger, and for good reason. If not done well, these relationships can go horribly wrong. Therefore, to engage young people in such questions takes courage and skill. Mentoring relationships evolve in much the same way that all truly beautiful relationships form, slowly over time, with a high degree of self-knowledge, relying on instinct and experience, adapting technique to particular personalities and environments, and trusting the process rather than focusing on outcome. Timing matters. To say to a young person, "I think God may be calling you to ordained ministry," may be overwhelming and even frightening if posed at the wrong moment, especially if the nineteen-year-old is simply trying to figure out what to major in and whether the attractive girl three rows over in biology even knows he exists. To ask the same question after the mentor has seen the mentee through some difficult stages, has seen her lead in campus worship, has engaged her in questions about scripture, purpose, and God, might be just the door needing to be opened.

Trust always matters. Even if a young person is willing to engage in more reflective processes and questions with a potential mentor, the quality of the conversation will deepen precisely in relationship to the depth of trust. In Antoine de Saint-Exupéry's classic children's story *The Little Prince*, the prince, the protagonist in the story, is befriended by a fox. The fox teaches the prince how to develop trust: "For me you are only a little boy just like a hundred thousand other little boys. And I have no need of you. And you have no need of me, either. But if you tame me we'll need each other. You'll be the only boy in the world for me and I'll be the only fox in the world for you."[1]

Anyone who has developed a profound friendship with another person knows trust, what the fox calls "taming," takes time to develop. Trust means consistency, content, and connection. Trust means always holding confidence and withholding judgment. Trust is gently lifting a mirror to another person so they see the beauty that is in them, and God's image shining from them, so that slowly over time they can learn to trust themselves. Without trust there can be little effective mentoring.

1. Saint-Exupéry, *Little Prince*, 59.

The great temptation of any of us who serve as a mentor is to remake the mentee in our own image, or to assume we know what is best for them. This temptation can be overpowering for some people, especially if the mentor and mentee already share similarities such as a common background and interests, personality, and intellectual curiosities. Excellent mentoring, like excellent spiritual direction, resists the urge to project one's own life story onto another, but rather calmly creates the space for the young person to discover his or her own desires, gifts, and insecurities, and opens a space to discover his or her deepest and truest self that is always the image of God already at work within. That's not to say a mentor should never give advice or tangible suggestions about decisions or opportunities the mentee may be wrestling with. Indeed, in my experience college students in particular often need tangible advice. However, the mentor should be ever vigilant that in giving such advice she is doing so always with the mentee's best interests in mind, and to the extent possible, avoiding the sneaky (and often hidden) impulse to live one's own life through the potential of another.

Encouraging college students to consider ordained ministry as a vocation takes thought and intentionality. The language mentors use matters. It shapes the world in which mentees come to understand themselves and their wider purpose. Mentor pastors should regularly talk about every Christian's call in baptism to take part in what God is doing in the world, the weighty responsibilities that come with discipleship, and the joy of being bound to one another in the church. They should pepper sermons and small-group discussions with references to the gifts God gives to each of us, and how those gifts can be used to build the kingdom, and the many scriptural passages in which Jesus beckons his disciples to follow. They should use language of "call," not only to ordained ministry, but to vocations in the secular world, and how being a disciple involves every aspect of one's life. Such vocabulary helps fuel the imagination of college students, explicitly pushing them to think and pray with a larger perspective, with eyes alert to where God is at work in the world, with hearts and hands receptive to the wonders of grace all around.

As a tangible example: Last spring I hosted a dinner for any student on the campus where I serve who might be interested in ordained ministry. I knew a handful would be there, but was pleasantly surprised when some twenty students showed up. Many of the students I knew, others I had never met. I learned a valuable lesson: talk about ministry, open the possibility, extend an invitation, allow the Spirit to work, assume students will be interested. I shared a little about my own path to ordained ministry and invited the students to talk about their own curiosity. The students were thoughtful and articulate young men and women from a range of Christian backgrounds. Each was relieved to discover they weren't the only one, that they now had a community of fellow travelers with whom to speak and pray.

I've found some specific practices to be helpful in encouraging students to explore ordained ministry. These are in addition to using a vocabulary of call and encouraging students to participate in historic Christian practices such as corporate worship, daily prayer and scripture reading, and engagement with the poor and forgotten.

Mentoring does not have to happen only in one-on-one relationships; it can also happen in small groups. For the last fifteen years I have led vocational discernment groups, small and welcoming communities where students can gather to read scripture, pray, listen to one another's lives, and talk about their emerging sense of call and where they imagine God might be leading them to serve. Students who later go into ordained ministry regularly name these moments of friendship and holy conversation as the starting point for their path to ministry. Such groups are successful to the extent that they meet routinely over a period of time (a semester or a year seem to work best), are of modest size (six to eight students is ideal), and develop enough trust that students feel free to speak openly. Leading such groups is different from teaching a class or Bible study. Leadership in this context requires a soft touch and involves framing appropriate themes through scripture and prayer, being consistent in meeting place and length of time, knowing when to speak, anticipating student voices, leaving room for silence, asking the right questions, and working to ensure a dynamic where all feel welcome. Often, students discover their deepest college friendships in such environments, and for some the groups take on a monastic and covenantal form.

A spiritual director once told me in the midst of a particularly angstridden time, "God comes to you in the disguise of your own life." This is another way of talking about incarnation. God is already at work in each of us, and in each college student. Vocation is the means by which God's on-going work in us becomes public. Thus, much of mentoring students is helping them tell the story of their own lives as a means of recognizing the good work God has already begun.

The philosopher Alasdair MacIntyre says that human beings are fundamentally narrative-based creatures. We are not a mere compilation of facts and figures. Rather, the shape of our lives is determined by character, plot, and drama expressed through particular lived experiences. Understanding narratives requires interpretive skill, historical analysis, and literary insight. Likewise, self-awareness necessitates probing beneath the depths, nosing out moments when the drama turns, patiently looking for patterns to emerge and previously invisible moments of significance to show themselves. The ability to tell stories, especially one's own story with honesty and nuance, does not happen all at once. It takes time, trial and error, testing out the plotlines with friends and family who know us well, patiently looking for a sense of coherence to develop.

This may sound simple, but it turns out learning to tell and interpret one's own story is extraordinarily difficult, particularly for young people who lack the advantage of perspective and life experience. The human capacity for self-deception is profound, and thus it is quite easy to simply tell stories that cast oneself as the hero or villain of the drama. But very often we are both hero and villain at the same time, the cause and effect of our personal fall and redemption. The temptation is to narrate our life in dissonant ways depending on the audience. For college students, one image emerges when surrounded by old high-school classmates, another appears in anthropology class, another emerges in mom's kitchen, and yet another comes to the fore in a job interview. On some level every story may well be a true account of who they are, and yet if they are to discover a cohesiveness that connects where they have been to who they are in the present to where they might be going, it is critical to be attentive, and look for the dominant themes that continue to appear, in the same way the primary melody of a song may be repeated over and over with different nuance throughout the score.

The themes that continue to reappear in our life story are the ones that require our deepest attention, and may serve as a kind of GPS to help navigate the future. I regularly push students to talk about their foundational stories: What are the narratives without which you would not be who you are? Almost always these involve relationships, family of origin, home town (or a lack of a place called home), particular friendships that have stood the test of time, public figures that have been role models, pastors and coaches with whom they develop a particular connection, interests that can be traced back to childhood and remain significant in college. These can serve as the DNA for discerning God's call, a direction for the future. Why have they been foundational? What is it about the magnetic pull of a particular friendship? The never-ending fascination with photography, or art, or insects, scripture, or architecture that continues to hold our attention? What aspects of our home town's culture, or the church of our youth, remain in our souls and shape the way we interact with every other community?

Learning to excavate and interpret our personal narratives is an essential skill for mentors and mentees alike, and there are tangible ways to learn and practice that skill. I have used the following three practices with college students.

Crafting a personal, one-sentence mission statement can be a helpful way to encourage students to explore vocation. It is incredibly difficult to take the vast scope, breadth, and complexity of one's life and put it down in one sentence. The mission should be broad enough to be energetic and aspirational, to involve a sense of value and purpose, yet focused enough to be tangible. Public and private-sector leaders have recognized the value of a clear and coherent mission statement for years as a way of organizing complex institutions with all the fiscal, capital, and human resources involved towards a common goal. Doing the same for one's own life can be a helpful way of framing the question: Why am I here? What am I really working towards in the big picture of my life? Who is God to me now?

I've discovered that many students have never thought about this before, often because no one has ever asked them to think about it and articulate it, and find the task enormously challenging. Many students are exhilarated by the exercise and engage it with diligence and passion. Other students are demoralized by the assignment, and often end up feeling frustrated because they have no idea what to say, or end up feeling sheepish or embarrassed because the best they have simply mimics the dominant narrative of success as accumulation, and the end game feels rather shallow. The point is not that one's purpose at nineteen or twenty is chiseled in rock, but rather to serve as a reflective moment, a touchpoint of self-evaluation, a coordinate on the map of one's emerging story. One student wrote, *My deepest purpose is to love and be loved by those around me, especially those no one else loves.* Another said, *I aspire for my spirit to resemble that of Christ and for my actions to meet the needs of his kingdom.* A third suggested, *I want to do justice, love kindness, and encourage others to do the same.* All of us should have such worthy dreams.

Second, write your own eulogy. The point here is to begin with the end in mind. When all is said and done, what do you want others to have said about you? How do you want to be seen by your friends and family, a child or spouse, a closest friend or colleague? What might it mean to live in such a way that one's eulogy that expresses the highest hopes for how you might be remembered, becomes a blue-print for how to live? Reading the self-written eulogies of college students regularly brings me to tears. I see in them a depth that is rarely displayed in the hyper-social consciousness of the modern college campus. The eulogies express profound values and ambition, hopes, fears, and aspirations. Once again, this is a devastatingly hard assignment for those who take it seriously. It involves confronting one's mortality, not an easy thing for a college sophomore, and explicitly saying what kind of person they want to become. Again, many students find it an affirming exercise, offering some assurance that they are on the right path. Others find it a painful process, recognizing the gap between who they are and who they genuinely aspire to be. The beauty of the process is that by recognizing that gap, they now might be motivated to close it, and they have articulated a vision of how they might do so.

Third, establish a clearness committee. One of the many gifts of the Quaker tradition is the belief that our truest self is often hidden and ever-changing, and we need to practice regular periods of silence to allow the external and internal noise to quiet so that we can truly listen to our interior lives and tell the story of our lives with integrity. The Quaker assumption is that we cannot do this alone. Rather, we need the presence of a wider community to help us listen and discern. The clearness committee is a way for one person to draw on the trust of close friends to help. The individual brings a significant question to the group: Should I take this new job? Should I get married? Should we have children? Should I pursue a new path? The role of the individual is to listen carefully and respond honestly, to trust him or herself, and those in the community completely. The role of the community is to ask clear and open questions and to withhold any advice or judgment, and to trust that in the process of silence, questions, listening, and responding, the person at the center of the circle will discern the right answer for him or herself. This process involves extraordinary levels of emotional and reflective vulnerability, and should only be practiced when a deep and shared trust and confidentiality exists within the group. It can, however, be an extremely helpful process for someone who is wrestling with a significant question or life choice. If a student is involved in a vocational discernment group or trusted Bible study, those groups might serve well in this process.

Geno Auriemma is perhaps the greatest women's basketball coach in NCAA history. He has been named national coach of the year multiple times and has won a bundle of national championships at the University of Connecticut. His UConn team beat Notre Dame to complete an undefeated season and win the 2015 national title. After the game he was asked what strategy he employed to beat such a good Notre Dame team. Auriemma said, "I have every confidence in my players and simply wanted them to play as themselves. I knew, though, at some point in the game they would need me, and when they did, I wanted to be there for them."

Too often mentors think they have to do things for their mentees. What mentees desperately need are mentors who encourage them to be who they are, and are prepared to be there for them when needed. The relationship does not end at graduation. I am in touch with baskets full of former students who have gone into all different kinds of professions, many of whom are in ordained ministry. I pray for them regularly and push myself to be there for them whenever possible. Sometimes these engagements have a tangible item attached: taking a look at an upcoming sermon, writing a letter of recommendation, or officiating a wedding. Mostly, however, the engagements are not to-do items: a note saying how much I believe in them, a phone call wondering how life is going, a text celebrating an accomplishment, a Facebook exchange maintaining contact.

The little prince tells the fox that "we are responsible forever for those we have tamed." Mentoring is not for the weak-kneed or faint of heart. Mentors are responsible forever for all who have entrusted their lives to our care. This is especially true for those who choose the path of ordained ministry. When a pastor is ordained, other clergy lay hands on her head, a sign of our apostolic lineage, the communion of the Spirit we share, and a symbol of the responsibility we who are farther down the ministry path have for those who are following. Therein lies the gift of mentoring, community, connection, friendship, love, which sounds a great deal like God.

We are all pilgrims, having been sent by God, we will return to God. The privilege of mentoring college students is the privilege of being a part of such a pilgrim life, to be there as it unfolds, to see where it might lead and be led, and to rejoice always, for the good work begun in each will be brought to completion in Jesus Christ.

# BIBLIOGRAPHY

Saint-Exupéry, Antoine de. *Little Prince*. Translated by Katherine Woods. New York: Harcourt, Brace & World, 1943.

# Chapter 11

# Kingdom Mentoring
## A Great Cloud of Witnesses

### SARAH S. HOWELL

WHEN I WAS ASKED to write for this book, I balked. "I complain constantly that I have had a hard time finding a mentor," I told Craig. "I have no idea what I would say." He said that's part of why I was being asked—that people need to hear what kind of mentoring a young pastor like me longs to receive.

So I sat down to make a wish list. I thought about all the things I would want in a mentor. Then I lamented that that person probably did not exist, and if she did, she would be way too busy or awesome to mentor me.

But then I found myself reflecting on people and communities that have influenced my life and as I've begun work in ministry. I realized that even though I have yet to find that one person at whose feet I can sit day and night and soak up wisdom, I have, indeed, been mentored—constantly, continually, and better than I have often realized.

I've started to do a little revisionism on my personal and pastoral history (however brief it may be yet), for I've come to see that there have already been many mentors who have shaped me—even when I did not know that's what was happening. More importantly, I'm seeing how I've been mentored not just or even primarily by individuals, but mostly within community; not always by those above me in some hierarchy of age or knowledge or professional experience, but often by peers and friends and the poor. I'm seeing, too, the mutuality and transformative power that often accompanies that exchange, qualities that must be at the forefront of mentoring for ministry in a time and place where what it looks like to be church is changing.

## 1. THE CROWD OF MENTORS

I have long lamented the fact that a person who fits all my criteria for a mentor has yet to appear in my life and offer to make me into the person and pastor I wish I were. As I think about it, though, it is ridiculous for me to expect that any one person could be everything I need in a mentor (as Jason Byassee points out in his mentoring essay).

Likely those unrealistic expectations of some mythical SuperMentor come from my own unrealistic expectations of myself as a person and as a pastor. Perhaps accepting that no one person can be everything to me is a good first step toward accepting that I cannot be everything to anyone else, either.

Rather, as I take a step back and look around, I find that although I have not had *a* mentor, I have had many, many mentors. The mentoring has come over time and in single interactions, from close relationships and from chance meetings—even, at times, from simply reading something that made me better.

The many individuals who have shaped my sense of call and pastoral identity have done so not mainly by telling me what to do but by giving me space to show up as my whole self, or by reflecting back the gifts and graces they see in me. This is probably a big part of why I often fail to recognize that mentoring is happening. I keep looking for someone to tell me what to do, when really what I need are opportunities to show up, the space to discover and use my gifts.

Looking over the extraordinary list of coauthors on this volume, I see varied examples of mentorship I have experienced. Both Craig and Jason have made room for me to question and wonder and even cry through crises of faith and call since I was a kid. Elaine's book *The Mystic Way of Evangelism* ruined my life for the better, and the first time we met, she caused me to reject and re-accept my call to ordained ministry, all in a twenty-four-hour period. Sam and I spent the same seven years at Duke, and his preaching and work continue to impact mine to this day. Jeremy is one of the holiest people I know, and I like to think that I get a little kinder every time I speak with him. I once sat in a clearness committee with Prince and grew by listening to his gentle questions and affirmation of the focus person. I met Melanie when we were on the staff of the Duke Youth Academy and was touched by her compassion and pursuit of wholeness. Will's writing and legacy saw me through seminary. Leighton's powerful witness to the strength of evangelical faith has influenced me by way of my father. James has contributed more to who I am as a person and as a pastor than anyone else ever has or ever will.

Now that I've started listing some of the individuals who make up this "crowd of mentors," I realize just how long the list is and how far back my crowd goes. As a child, I took for granted what a rock star my mom was in her work with the sick and dying, the poor and disenfranchised, and I marvel at it now. My maternal grandfather showed me what it looked like to lead as a pastor and a Methodist bishop with grace and intentionality. My maternal grandmother, the daughter of a Southern Baptist preacher and a pioneer in liturgical and modern dance (go figure), knows Jesus better than anyone I've ever met and prays for me daily. My 4th grade teacher, Heather Smith, inspired an early love of the natural sciences that crops up in my preaching and teaching even now. My middle-school choir teacher, Treda Berry, insisted that we memorize our music, a skill that to this day makes me an obnoxious hymn-singer (because I rarely need the hymnal). My high-school choir director, Joyce Palmieri, kept us to a practice of praying before concerts that somehow felt inclusive even of non-believers. Oscar Dantzler, the housekeeper at Duke Chapel (who I believe does more pastoral care than anyone else on Duke's campus), was a listening ear while I was discerning field-education opportunities that I felt would shape my life and ministry for years to come.

No one of these people could have given me everything I need in a mentoring relationship. But together, over time, in a variety of places and ways and to different degrees, these and many others have mentored me more fully than my imaginary SuperMentor could have done. I have needed each one of them individually, and I have needed all of them together, to become who I am today—and I've only just begun.

## 2. MENTORING IN COMMUNITY

A crowd is not the same thing as a community. Although some of the individuals I named above are connected, many of them have never met and probably never will. Many come from very different stages in my life, different spheres of my ministry and vocation. Although they are as an aggregate my community (or at least a part of it), they are not necessarily community with one another in the way I have found I most need it.

As an undergraduate student studying religion while deeply involved in campus ministry, I was influenced by Shane Claiborne and the Simple Way, by Jonathan Wilson-Hartgrove and the Rutba House, and by the idea of intentional Christian community. I continue to learn that the reality is much more difficult than the idea.

In the summer of 2008, I participated in a program for Duke undergraduates where 6 of us lived in a house in Durham's West End neighborhood for a summer and worked in the community and shared life together. My senior year of college, I was one of eight members of the Duke Wesley Fellowship that shared a house on the edge of East Campus. This experience brought my idealism around intentional community back to earth and taught me to work with and within the community that exists, not an ideal I might impose from theory.

I spent all three years of seminary living in an intentional community with a rotating cast of five or six other people, an experience that was beautiful and hard and life-giving and exhausting. Leigh, Brandon, Jesse, Samuel, Christian, and Milton loved me, challenged me, supported me, and drove me crazy through seminary and field education, breakups and breakdowns, and my own stubborn resistance to community life.

When I moved to Winston-Salem, North Carolina, in 2012, I was twenty-five years old and had never lived by myself. In fact, I had gotten to the point where I felt like I had lived too much with other people. I wanted nothing more than to have my own space, finally, and thereby, I thought, to grow up.

So I found a 600-square-foot apartment on the edge of downtown Winston-Salem and settled in to adult life. I was independent and grown up.

I was also deeply lonely. My grandparents had been in Winston about a year and were a wonderful support (my grandmother brought me chicken-noodle soup once when I was sick—I seriously did not know what to do when I had a cold and was by myself), but something was missing. As I struggled into my new role as a pastor, I felt the lack of people to care for and about me as a person.

About a month into my time in Winston, I noticed a cardboard encampment across the street from my church. Curious, I wandered over. There I found a ragtag bunch of people praying compline from *Common Prayer: A Liturgy for Ordinary Radicals*,[1] accompanied by ukulele and mostly bad singing. I couldn't tell who at this Festival of Shelters (or Sukkot) were members of Anthony's Plot Community and who were the local homeless joining them for food and shelter and solidarity, but I quickly realized that was the point. Anthony's Plot, an intentional Christian community, covenants with the Sunnyside neighborhood and with all vulnerable peoples of Winston-Salem, including primarily the homeless population, for mutual support and relational uplift.

I was so annoyed. I thought I had left intentional community in Durham, yet here it was—welcoming me and forcing me to admit that I needed it still.

A year later, I had moved into the Sunnyside neighborhood, just around the corner from Anthony's Plot (I was just "community adjacent," unwilling to move back into full-time residential community). It was, for me, an experiment in the radical interdependency that community embodies. The house and I shared a lawnmower and tools, keys to our houses, meals and game nights and worship and prayer.

The same resistance I had manifested in the house I lived in during seminary cropped back up, and every now and then I would step away for a while. I didn't like how Anthony's Plot challenged my dependence on material goods, how they made me spend a lot of time with people I wouldn't normally choose to hang out with, how their work pressed up against my personal and pastoral anxieties. I didn't like how their desire to do good trampled all over my focus on doing things perfectly.

The beauty of individual mentors is that you can take what you like and leave the rest. In an actual community—not just a crowd—it becomes a little more difficult to pick and choose, especially if you covenant with that community or share life with them in some way. The community, more so than the crowd, has shown me that often to be mentored well is to be challenged and changed.

---

1. Claiborne, Wilson-Hartgrove, and Okoro, *Common Prayer*.

## 3. MENTORING AMONG EQUALS

When I got past my SuperMentor archetype and started to appreciate the many ways in which I have been mentored without realizing it, I found something unexpected. Certainly most of the people I would count as mentors in my life have been older and wiser. Right now, however, most of the best mentoring I get is from peers, not superiors.

As a United Methodist pastor, I experience both the joy and the burden of our connectional system. There's bureaucracy, sure, but there is also a vast network of incredibly gifted and hilarious people. These people are all over the spectrum in terms of age, but in my conference, the young clergy in particular have taught me a great deal about ministry, not because they are older or more experienced than I, but because we have committed to learning and growing together.

As our denomination wrestles with questions about human sexuality and inclusion, some of my peers have wondered if we might have a different conversation. Across our conference, small groups of young clergy have been getting together to ask questions and build relationships around these difficult topics. Instead of debating the finer points of *The Book of Discipline* and legislation for General Conference, we have asked one another where we see pain and where we see hope in these conversations.

At Annual Conference last year, some of the leaders of these talks decided to embody the spirit of unity they are intended to express by going as a group—a group of differing opinions and beliefs and yet with a shared love of the church and one another—to both the Evangelical Prayer Breakfast (symbolic, in our minds, of a more conservative caucus) and the Reconciling Worship Service (symbolic of a more progressive group). I'm sure certain members of our posse were ogled as potential spies at each of these events, but we went to pray, to worship, to listen, and to be together.

This group of young clergy has helped to pull me out of the anger and frustration that bubbles up in me when controversial topics tear at the seams of the church I love. In a non-hierarchical, mutual way, they have imparted a great deal of wisdom, patience, and love.

Sometimes, too, my peers—whether ministerial or social—are better equipped to recognize and meet my immediate needs because theirs are similar. I think of one week after the Wednesday-night worship service we have at my church. Worship had ended, and people were milling about, some leaving, some staying to chat, several waiting to speak with me. As I talked to a congregant about the sermon, I felt a gentle but insistent tug on my arm and turned to see my fiancé, Colin, beckoning me to the side.

A glimmer of irritation came and went—clearly I was still working, so to speak, but he wouldn't have stepped in if it weren't important. So I went with him, and he led me over to the communion table.

"You forgot to take communion," he said, and offered me the bread and the cup with a tender smile.

I was floored. Indeed, I had been so focused on serving the sacrament to everyone else that I had neglected to receive it myself.

My peers are sometimes better attuned and equipped to care for me in a way that allows me to show up as fully myself and to encounter God when I am too busy to notice the movement of the Spirit around me.

## 4. MENTORING WITH THE OTHER

I first wandered into Asbury Temple United Methodist Church in Durham, North Carolina, when I was barely nineteen, a freshman college student seeking a different worship experience. Asbury Temple felt like the kingdom to me: a predominantly African-American church with a smattering of white congregants; a place where worship was both deeply liturgical and profoundly Spirit-led; a gathering of people of diverse socioeconomic and educational backgrounds brought together to bear witness to Christ in Northeast Central Durham, a neighborhood the police referred to as the Bullseye, where poverty and crime were visible.

I spent the next two years mostly worshipping in the back and not much else. Even in this passive role, I was taught a great deal about community, justice, and race. But the real mentoring came when I got involved with a new summer camp effort that was a collaboration among several churches of different racial backgrounds. Between two summers of working at The Wright Room (the summer camp named after a matriarch of Asbury Temple) and a subsequent year of serving as the youth minister at the church, I was mentored primarily by children and youth to whom my long, blonde hair was a novelty.

Hannah Bonner, then a Duke Divinity School student, handed me Toni Morrison's *Bluest Eye* as required summer reading. I began to wrestle with white privilege in a new way. I encountered cultural differences and social anxieties. And I was cared for and loved by people who had no reason to do so other than the fact that I continued to show up. The pastor there offered me the pulpit and entrusted me with the wellbeing of the youth and children of the congregation. I was mentored by the leaders and the members (even the youngest among them) simply by being made a minority for the first time.

Since Asbury Temple, I have needed opportunities to be with and learn from people who are not like me. As a fresh-faced pastor in a new town, I stumbled into membership in the Ministers' Conference of Winston-Salem and Vicinity, a historically African-American clergy organization. When I was asked to lead a community vigil after the Charleston shooting, they came to my aid, and the president, Bishop Todd Fulton, spoke hard truths—gently—when I fumbled on how to help a white church respond.

Most recently, I have found myself leading a support group for people living with HIV, something I know nothing about. The clients of AIDS Care Service come from all different backgrounds, but they are mostly poor and mostly black. It is with the wonderful people of ACS that I have experienced some of the sharpest growing pains in the last year. I thought I knew a little something about poverty and race—perhaps I had grown cocky as a white woman who'd attended a black church for a while. But with ACS, I keep being surprised by how the things I say or do offend or fall flat because of social and cultural differences I never saw coming. The clients have not sugarcoated things for me, but they have loved me all the same, embodying a community of the other that is mentoring me in ways that I know will bear deep-rooted fruit in due time.

There is some aspect of mentoring that requires connection and familiarity. Certainly my idea of a SuperMentor looks something like a new and improved me. But in allowing myself to be taught and shaped by the other, by the poor, by men and women whose experience is radically different than mine but whose blood runs just as red, I am gaining something so much more profound than if I had a WASP-y woman mentor who grew up in a college town like I did.

## 5. HOSPITALITY AND MENTORING

The Latin word for "host" is *hospes*. *Hospes* can also be translated "guest." In many ways, the terms "mentor" and "mentee" can be so interchangeable when the relationship is truly fruitful—both parties in need of wisdom and insight, a space to show up as their whole selves.

I will not be the only contributor to this volume to lift up the mutuality of the mentor-mentee relationship. Willimon points out that the mentor, not just the mentee, must be prepared to learn.

But this reminder need not be so remarkable. The analogy of hospitality, particularly as understood by the Benedictines, is instructive. The Rule of St. Benedict, with the robust support of Scripture, exhorts adherents to welcome any visitor as if he or she were Christ. This isn't just a nice thought—it's a reality of recognizing the divine image in the other, of remembering that Christ dwells in all people, that all are children of God, beloved by God, and that to reject any one of those children is to reject Christ.

Social norms might lead us to elevate the role of the host over the guest, but the witness of Scripture and the etymology of the words themselves crack open a very different reality. Both host and guest are mutually received and accepted, both open to transformation and growth, both in need and also with much to offer. So it is for mentors and mentees. The mentee seeks a mentor who has something he or she doesn't have but wants—and the mentor finds in the mentee something that he or she lacks as well. In each welcoming the other, each coming to the other with much to give and much to learn, a mutual exchange occurs where lines between host and guest, mentor and mentee, are blurred to the benefit of all involved.

To return to our Latin lesson, *hospes* not only means both "host" and "guest" but also comes from the root *hostis*, meaning "enemy." Odd how seeming antonyms are so closely related etymologically. But perhaps the one who is hospitable to me becomes an enemy to my idolatry of self. One who approaches me as a guest in need of welcome does so even more radically, forcing me to put their needs before my own—and thereby redefining what I think I "need."

In the same way, the mutuality of a mentor-mentee relationship of any kind breaks down barriers between and within people. Mentoring is the enemy of self-involvement, both the self-congratulatory kind and the self-deprecating kind.

Henri Nouwen, a man I count among my crowd of mentors despite the fact that he passed away when I was nine years old, has this to say in his book *The Wounded Healer*: "The great illusion of leadership is to think that man can be led out of the desert by someone who has never been there."[2] This illusion is twofold: one, that a mentee might seek a mentor he or she

2. Nouwen, *Wounded Healer*, 78.

thinks has everything perfectly together; and two, a mentor might presume he or she can speak wisdom from on high without revealing the truth of struggle and difficulty that has accompanied his or her learning and growth.

But the host is lonely without the guest, and the guest has nowhere to go without the host. The mentor is not a mentor without a mentee, and vice versa. And none of us can be brothers and sisters in Christ, ministers or laity, leaders or followers, teachers or students one without the other. We cannot take anyone else where we ourselves have not gone, and we cannot go much of anywhere alone.

Mentoring for ministry in a church seeking to bear witness in a changing world must be based not on method or hierarchy but on mutually uplifting relationship enabled by the Spirit. Mentoring should not be tied to any one strategy or theory of leadership or organizational management. Instead, it must embrace the diversity, mutuality, community, and hospitality that will surely be represented when the kingdom comes in full.

## BIBLIOGRAPHY

Claiborne, Shane, Jonathan Wilson-Hartgrove, and Enuma Okoro. *Common Prayer: A Liturgy for Ordinary Radicals*. Grand Rapids: Zondervan, 2010.
Nouwen, Henri J. M. *The Wounded Healer: Ministry in Contemporary Society*. Garden City, NY: Doubleday, 1972.

# Inconclusive Conclusion

## Martin E. Marty

The editors and this author conceived of this chapter first as a Foreword and later as an Afterword. Think of it as a conclusion, because no other chapters follow it. But not only did my colleagues with whom I keep company between the covers of this book not license me to conceive of this as a cutting-off of their work and helping the publisher and editor set it free from its manuscripted context—the spirit of all the authors and the chapters, sometimes explicitly stated, celebrates growth, change, and openness to a variety of alternatives within the mentor/mentee relationships. Several make a point of the concept of conversation. Stop here, for a moment to consider that.

One of my mentors has been longtime University of Chicago colleague David Tracy. My campus study adjoined his, and for several years it was figuratively and—quite possibly—literally true that I was picking up new influences from his world by sensing vibrations from what he was formally imparting to students or picking up from them or from guests who made a way to his door. The reason I had to qualify the word about the influence of vibrations is because contributor William Willimon strongly stresses the importance of words in mentorial transactions. No doubt, what I learned did come from words, as we met on the stairs or as we opened our doors and, let's be realistic, over coffee or once when we co-taught a course.

What mentor Tracy transmitted most usefully in some definitions within his writings and consistently in his bearing and speech is a distinction between argument and conversation. Argument is framed in the setting of a contention: one participant in an exchange proposes a thesis that she must defend or use to convince or defeat the other. There are winners and losers and, note well, conclusions. Argument is extremely valuable in legislatures, laboratories, and treatises. One hopes that all mentors can capably argue, to effect certain ends. But there are limits.

If arguments are framed by remembered or proposed answers, good conversations thrive on questions. Several authors on these pages stress the importance of listening, on the part of both (or more) participants in a conversation. In a sense, these do not end, because, if they are lively and engaging and deep, they lead to more lively and engaging and deep words. The stress on conversation, openness, and change in mentoring contexts is what led me to be qualify the naming of the conclusion of this book as *inconclusive*.

Mentoring, as demonstrated in these chapters, is always case-specific and culture-specific. "Case" can sound cold or formal, as in the "case" of legal and medical interactions. By this point in this book, however, we can trust that every author regards mentors as specific persons and personalities. They are not interchangeable or dissolvable into some generic idea of mentor-hood. They all know that a vast literature about mentoring exists in schools of management or higher education. These are usually of the "How to Mentor" variety, in which, characteristically, we read lists of "Ten Steps to Effective Mentoring" or "Every Would-be Mentor Prosper If . . ." There are only a couple of listings and categorizations in this book and they passed the editorial tests of appearing within narrative or personal homiletic expressions.

"Cases," also in medicine and law, are, at their best, short-hand expressions of access to or summary about real persons. For practical reasons of efficiency, a person in a specific ward may be thought of as a "case," but her good physician knows that she is suffering from terminal cancer, and must be addressed and treated in the context of that terror. In law, a "case" may be a person just released from a prison term, and can be thought of as a new being. His attorney may refer to "the case of the innocently imprisoned Mr. Jones," but if that attorney is any good, he was moved beyond law or bank ledgers and grown close to a person in agony and, in the end, one hopes in ecstasy.

Whoever has read these chapters and now, in this hour of celebrated inconclusivity, scans and revisits any or all of them, will know how specific virtually all references to mentoring issue from recall and observation of this or that saint (e.g., Augustine or Paul or a less well-known "saintly" teacher or coach) who exemplified certain virtues or who made demands that would inspire growth. As we will mention later, often these relate to specific vocations or assignments related to the world of the mentored one.

Mentoring is not only case-specific, it is also culture-specific. Cultures are assemblages of terms, gestures, traditions, expressions, shared by others within a specific setting. They can be defined so narrowly and sharply that they will blunt the allure and promise of neighboring or overlapping cultures. (We are all "plural-belongers" to cultures, a fact that irritates cultists, who shun or expel those who import traits from others.) This book's intent is not to build walls and boundaries and pulpits-for-boasting. They are in a Christian cultural tradition that is Catholic, which means—in the etymological reference to *kata olos*, embracing the whole, or ecumenical, which refers to the larger household of a faith community.

Editor Byassee acknowledged to me what led him to seem a bit uneasy or apologetic, but which appealed to me: most of the authors relate "catholicly" and "ecumenically" to a major Protestant culture, often called Wesleyan, to honor its Anglo-lineage traceable to a major reformer, John Wesley. I don't find any contributors here to be confined by a broad Wesleyan heritage. It helps one to locate the authors and the conversationalists. At the same time, most of what is here, because of its roots in the Jesus experience and movement, mentors like the Apostle Paul are taken more or less for granted as an exemplar.

I say "more or less" because all the authors assume that there will be and should be changes within "their" culture. Women in the Wesleyan and other Protestant traditions, and certainly in the Augustinian inheritance, have undertaken to effect revision, change, and renewal in their tradition, as some chapters in this book make clear.

This inconclusive conclusion is not a license for me to turn didactic and wrap knuckles or make noise on the blackboard for readers to listen to me and my snatchings from the assemblage of ideas and events that make up the Lutheran culture within Protestantism that is kin to the Wesleyan. My mission and assignment here is to listen to what is said, to notice what one might overlook, to learn from mentors as here described and to encourage ever more catholic and ecumenical encounters and experiences.

I used these chapters as mirrors to hold up and reveal what I had not noticed before, where I fell short of the promise of mentorship as it can be at its best. Like many other readers, I find the call to change difficult. Richard Hooker, an Anglican divine, mentored me with his observation that "all change is inconveniencing, including from worse to better." And paraphrases of John Newman survive to inspire, as when he reminds us that to grow is to change and to grow much means to have changed often and much.

One cannot read these chapters without noticing how often the relation to and the choice of a mentor falls to chance. It even gets called "lucky" on these pages. Notice of that leads me once more to what I learned from David Tracy. He taught me somewhere and somehow that one cannot face the fullness of humanity, or exemplify faith, hope, and love, without coming to terms with three basic features in the human condition: finitude, contingency, and transience. I asked him for a citation from his works, so I could reference it, but he couldn't come up with it. (Maybe a reader of this book can, and will oblige.) Instead, he said those three themes color all his work (and mine, and, dear reader, yours).

Finitude: we and all things will die. Transience: nothing temporal lasts. And in the middle is contingency, the realm of accidents and surprises and mutual dependences, and luck. So it is luck (or providence, or Providence) that positions us to the conversations with true mentors, who are often surprised to find who their true mentees are. Sarah Howell here talks of a crowd, whose members we can conceive of as possibilities. Take your choice, or find yourself chosen, a word you'll find in the mentee context here.

Two notes remain: one is the reminder that James Howell suggested, that books can be mentors. Machiavelli changed his dusty or muddy Florentine street clothes to "garments regal and courtly" when he entered his library to spend an evening with the great writers and teachers and, yes, mentors. The other note points to the value of humor in mentor–mentee relations. Teaching can be argumentative without ever being conversational, hierarchical and authoritarian without being personal. If we could convoke all the authors in this book and ask them about the lighter side of their relation to their mentors, we would likely find that many would reference the generous humor of many of their mentors.

One illustration might suffice. I am in the larger Lutheran culture, in which many teachers through the past five centuries have chosen to teach dogmatically, grimly. You can attend many conferences of Lutherans who converge on their main theme, justification by grace through faith, only to find them often being graceless while trying to be faithful. They can argue endlessly about the finest points of what justification should mean, but where do these lead? Martin Luther admitted that he hated to preach on this key doctrine, the article of faith on which the church stands or falls. He staked his life and teaching on that doctrine, but when he tried to preach on it he failed. The congregation members would fall asleep or otherwise lose interest. Did he give up the teaching? No he mentored the people by his choice to tell stories, which led to the preferred outcome: they listened and were changed.

So I close with a story of mentorship by reference to Johannes Staupitz, remembered in this book as mentor to Luther in his crucial stage. Luther, moving to reform, was living in the context of legalistic catholic cultural norms. Confession of sin was at the heart of his way to experience the grace of God. So he confessed and confessed and confessed to his confessor Staupitz, whom I would have favored as my mentor if given the chance. But Staupitz, an ordained listener, knew limits. As he had to sit for hours listening to Luther being hyper-scrupulous and searching and gabby, his patience wore out, and in one remembered counsel made the real point of Christian confession by negative reference: "Martin, you don't have to confess every fart." I hope that crude bit from Lutheran mentor-culture translates effectively to Wesleyan and other Christian cultures where mentorship faces many trials, but often wins.

Made in the USA
Middletown, DE
12 June 2023

32457380R00080